ROMANTIC
COMEDY

ROMANTIC COMEDY

Bernard Slade

NELSON DOUBLEDAY, INC.
Garden City, New York

ROMANTIC COMEDY opened in New York at the Ethel Barrymore Theater on November 8, 1979. It was directed by Joseph Hardy. Scenery was by Douglas W. Schmidt; costumes by Jane Greenwood; and lighting by Tharon Musser. Production stage manager was Warren Crane. It was presented by Morton Gottlieb; Ben Rosenberg and Warren Crane associate producers, in association with Thornhill Productions, Inc.

The cast in order of appearance was:

Jason Carmichael	Anthony Perkins
Blanche Dailey	Carole Cook
Phoebe Craddock	Mia Farrow
Allison St. James	Holly Palance
Leo Janowitz	Greg Mullavey
Kate Mallory	Deborah May

ROMANTIC COMEDY

SETTING

The entire action of the play takes place in the study of Jason Carmichael's New York townhouse.

ACT ONE

Scene 1: A spring morning in the mid-sixties.
Scene 2: Late night, a year later.

ACT TWO

Scene 1: A November morning, ten years later.
Scene 2: Late afternoon, six weeks later.

ACT THREE

Scene 1: A mid-September morning, two years later.
Scene 2: Late afternoon, three weeks later.
Scene 3: The next morning.

ACT ONE

Scene 1

TIME: A spring morning in 1965.

SETTING: The spacious study of Jason Carmichael's New York
            townhouse. The back wall contains a window that
            looks out onto the garden, there are double doors stage
            left that lead to the hall and a door stage right leads
            to a non-visible dressing room. The room is furnished
            with the usual number of sofas, chairs, coffee and end
            tables, and there is an antique desk upstage center that
            contains some neatly stacked scripts, papers, a tele-
            phone and a covered typewriter. Some of the walls are
            booklined and the study projects an aura of warm,
            tasteful, traditional elegance.

AT RISE: The phone is ringing in the unoccupied room. After a
            moment, Jason Carmichael enters from the dressing
            room. He is, as always, impeccably attired, at the
            moment in a dressing gown, ascot, slacks and velvet
            slippers. He is carrying a well tailored blue suit. At this
            point in time, in his mid-thirties, he is not conven-
            tionally handsome but, despite his crumpled face,
            possesses a mixture of arrogance, charm and sophistica-
            tion that gives him a certain magnetism.

JASON
(Irritably muttering to himself)
I really wish someone would get that.

(Apparently someone does, as the phone stops ringing. Blanche Dailey opens the double doors and pokes her head into the room. Flamboyant in manner and dress, she admits to forty-two, looks fiftyish, is actually fifty-seven. Texas-born, thrice married, an ex-showgirl, but for many years a literary agent, she is nobody's fool)

BLANCHE
(Surprised)
Why aren't you dressed?

JASON
My club's sending Boris—or someone over to give me a rubdown.

(She enters, closing doors behind her)

BLANCHE
Isn't that a bit redundant on your wedding day? What are you doing holed up in here anyway?

JASON
Allison's parents and some of her assorted relatives are staying in the upstairs rooms so I've been sleeping in the dressing room. How's the house?

BLANCHE
Filling up. And, at the risk of introducing a somber note into this festive affair, costing you a bundle you can ill afford.

JASON
(Quietly)
God, you're crass.

BLANCHE
(Unmoved)
I'm supposed to be. I'm your agent.
(Looking at suits)
You know your problem, Jason? You came out of your mother's womb yelling "I'll take one in every color."

JASON
What do you want? You have an ulterior look about you.

BLANCHE

Well, for one thing, I wanted to audition the costume.
(She does a model's twirl)
Very restrained for an old Follies girl, right?

JASON

Blanche, you have a choice. You can either be a Follies girl or you can be forty-two years old. You cannot be both.

BLANCHE

I hate people with mathematical minds.
(The phone rings and Blanche picks it up. Into phone)
Jason Carmichael's residence—Yes, he is—Oh—Hold on a minute, please.
(She holds out the phone to him)
Long distance.

(He takes phone. She moves to pour herself a drink)

JASON

(Into phone)
Yes?
(His tone changes)
Oh, hello—No, you're not the *last* person I expected to hear from but I have had more thrilling beginnings to my day—Yes, I got your messages—Because, frankly, I didn't see any point in talking to you.
(Becoming agitated)
Look, you were the one who walked out, not me!—It wasn't what you did, it was the way you did it. If you'd been open with me instead of sneaking around behind—Oh, come on, you'd been meeting with him for over three months. Christ, we were together for *eleven* years and I had to find out by reading it in a column!
(He regains some control)
I agree. No point at all so I'm going to hang up now. I have a very busy schedule today—I'm going to have a massage and then get married—Well, maybe someday we'll be able to sit down and laugh over it but I think you should know I don't plan on ever becoming that mellow.
(Very upset, he hangs up and turns to look at Blanche)

BLANCHE

Marty?

JASON

Can you imagine the gall of that man? After all that's happened?

BLANCHE

Jason, he was your writing partner, not your wife. You sound like a jilted lover.

JASON

Why shouldn't I feel jilted? The man was meeting with some film producer behind my back working on a *screenplay!*

BLANCHE

I'm sure he wanted you to work on it with him but he knew you'd never move to L.A.

JASON

I'm too young to start writing about real life from memory.

BLANCHE

Since when did you write about real life?

JASON
(Pacing—very agitated)
My God, do you know what I went through with that man for eleven years? He always exuded a strange musty smell that positively made your head reel. Did you ever notice that?

BLANCHE

You'll find someone else.

JASON
(A sudden change of mood; sadly)
No, I'll never find another partner like Marty. Why did he do it, Blanche?

BLANCHE
(Shrugs)
Oh, I don't know—I always got the feeling Marty felt overshadowed by you. Maybe he just wanted his own identity.

JASON

Who could confuse us? The man was five feet tall and had a small clump of hair growing out of the bridge of his nose.

(She watches him as he moves to pour himself a healthy drink)

BLANCHE

I sense a certain panic in you, Jason. What is it?

(He turns to look at her)

JASON

Marty and I spent all our writing lives together. Together we had five smash hits, two nervous hits and one flop. Lately, I've had this persistent, nasty little thought.
(He looks at her; simply)
Was he the talented one?

(Blanche is too astounded by his uncharacteristic vulnerability to reply)
Blanche, this is no time for a pause.

BLANCHE

I always get tongue-tied when I discover someone's human.

JASON

If you let it get outside this room I'll tell everyone that's the real color of your hair.

(They embrace. He moves away)
Where the hell is Boris? I have a knot in my shoulder that feels as if it was tied by a stevedore.

BLANCHE

You found anyone else you think you can work with?

JASON

Blanche, it's not like hiring a maid! A collaboration is a very sensitive relationship. It has all the disadvantages of a marriage and none of the advantages.

BLANCHE

What did you think of this play I sent you—*The Girl In The Back Seat?*

JASON

Oh, I don't know—I only half read it—I suppose it has a certain quaint charm, but I'm in no mood to make any decisions right now.

BLANCHE

Well, I think it has great possibilities and the author wanted you to read it. His name is P. J. Craddock.

JASON

What kind of name is that?

BLANCHE

Probably a real one. We've just corresponded so I don't know a damn thing about him except that he teaches school somewhere up in Vermont. Look, why don't you take the script along on your honeymoon? It'll help fill in the awkward pauses. The author's coming into town a week from today and I've set up a meeting with him here at eleven o'clock. Okay?

JASON

What makes you think we'll have awkward pauses?

BLANCHE

What? Oh, just a figure of speech.

JASON

I thought you liked Allison.

BLANCHE

I adore Allison.

JASON

Did I tell you her father was the Ambassador to New Zealand?

BLANCHE

Not in the last ten minutes. Why are you so impressed?

JASON

Blanche, the man has a *flag* on his car.

BLANCHE

Is that why you're getting married, Jason? So you can doublepark in downtown Auckland?

JASON

(After a slight pause)
Allison has some rare qualities, you know. She's unspoiled, sweet, giving, spontaneous. All the things I'm not.

BLANCHE

Honest, but hardly a reason for marriage.

JASON

All right. I'll be thirty-five next month. I want a family before I get too old.
(A slight shrug)
The timing's right.

BLANCHE

It's still not too late to call the whole thing off and send everyone home, you know.

JASON

Just like in *The Philadelphia Story*? People don't do that in real life.

(Blanche stands)

BLANCHE

Well—if there's not going to be any drama I may as well get drunk.
(She moves to the door)

JASON

Tell the maid to keep everyone out of here, will you? The only person I want to see is a masseur.

BLANCHE

Jason, are you *sure* you want to go through with this?

JASON

Of course I'm not. Is anybody just before their wedding?
(A beat)
But I'm sure of one thing. This marriage is going to work.

BLANCHE

How do you know?

JASON

I'm a perfectionist.

(She looks at him for a moment)

BLANCHE

(Gently)

Break a leg, kid.

(She exits.

Jason stands for a moment before he exits to the dressing room leaving the suit on the chair at stage left.

After a moment, the double doors open and Phoebe enters. She is holding an overstuffed, scuffed tote purse. We will later see that she is quite pretty but if Jason has made the best of his looks, she has made the worst. At this point in her mid-twenties she is inclined to cover her basic shyness with a somewhat self-conscious forthright manner. Right now she is totally overawed by her surroundings and stands drinking in the room. After a few moments she summons up enough courage to move back to the desk, tentatively touches the manuscripts. Finally, she slowly sits, not quite believing she is sitting at Jason Carmichael's desk. The phone rings. She stands and stares at it)

JASON (Offstage)

I'd really appreciate it if someone would get that.

(She gulps and picks up phone)

PHOEBE

(Into phone)

Hello—Yes, it is—Boris called in with the flu and can't come—Yes, I'll—I'll pass on that message.

(She hangs up. At this point Jason enters from the dressing room. He is totally nude. Oblivious to Phoebe, who is in a frozen state of shock, Jason carries a portable massage table which partially shields his body from the audience. He turns upstage, and moves towards the desk but stops in his tracks as he sees Phoebe. His back is now three-quarters to the audience, she is behind the desk, facing the audience; staring fixedly at Jason's hairline, trying to appear unruffled. There is a pause)

JASON

(Calmly)
Where's Boris?

PHOEBE

Oh, Boris couldn't come.

JASON

Oh.

(A pause)

PHOEBE

I'm—overawed.

(Another pause)

JASON

(Finally)
Thank you.

PHOEBE

You're younger looking than your photos.
(Too brightly)
Of course most of those were head shots. Ha, ha. What a dumb thing to say! I have this cousin who writes me letters and always puts "ha-ha" after anything she means to be funny. May I ask a question?

JASON

Of course.

PHOEBE

Are you naked?

JASON

Either that or I'm standing in a very severe draft.

PHOEBE

You're just a white blob to me. I'm not wearing my glasses. I have very weak eyes.

JASON

Well, I hope you have strong hands.

PHOEBE

Strong hands?

JASON

I have a knot in my shoulder. Do you think you can do anything about it?

PHOEBE

Well—I don't know. I can try—
       (She speaks in an even stream of words)
—but first I'd like to say that I've seen all your plays and admired your work for many years. In fact, at the risk of sounding gushy, I might say I've idolized your talent. Over the years you and your partner have brightened one's days, molded one's tastes, and although impossible to attain, provided one with a standard of civilized behavior.

       (There is a longish pause)

JASON

       (Finally)
You're not the masseur.

PHOEBE

You thought I was?

JASON

I rarely receive guests in the buff.

PHOEBE

I'm very relieved to hear that. I mean I'm trying to appear unruffled and chic but underneath I'm a terrible prude.

JASON

Look, I don't want to appear churlish but I'm getting rather chilly. Who are you?

PHOEBE

Oh, I'm *The Girl In The Back Seat.*
(A beat)
P.J. Craddock. But my given name is Phoebe.

JASON

You're a week early.

PHOEBE

No, it's today.
(Happy to get out of his line of vision she moves around to
extract a letter from her purse. He does not move)
I have the letter right here. It's a bit grubby from constant reading
but—here.
(She hands it to him. He glances at it)

JASON

Uh—would you excuse me for a moment?

(In a flurry of activity, she quickly gathers up her purse)

PHOEBE

Gladly!
(She makes for the door, stops, awkwardly tries to lighten the
situation)
It's funny, one's fantasies never turn out quite how one expects, do
they? I mean, I'd always visualized you wearing a sports coat.
(She makes a rather awkward exit.

Jason puts the letter on the sofa, very calmly puts on his
shorts, and shirt, and crosses to the mirror. He is looking into
the mirror when his calm exterior shatters)

JASON

That—was—the—most—*embarrassing experience of my life!!!*
(He lets out an anguished yell and, overcome by the embarrassment of it all, proceeds to go into a jerky, strange, mania-
cal, hopping series of movements or dance around the room,
all the time muttering)
God—that was embarrassing! Totally—embarrassing! Standing there
naked like an idiot—*embarrassing!* Completely and utterly—
(He stops as he sees that Phoebe, clutching her purse has

opened the door and is staring at him; an odd expression on her face)

PHOEBE

I'm sorry. I thought I heard you yelling as if you were in pain.

JASON

(Extremely calm and polite again)

No, I'm all right, thank you.

PHOEBE

Oh. Well, excuse me again.
(She exits.

Jason looks heavenward for a moment before letting out a low, heartfelt expletive)

JASON

Oh—shit!!
(He pulls himself together, puts on trousers, and crosses to doors and opens them to admit Phoebe)

PHOEBE

Look, perhaps I should come back at the Easter break.

JASON

(Drily)

Why? We're having so much fun.

PHOEBE

Well, they seem to be preparing for some sort of function out there.

JASON

I'm sorry, Miss Craddock, I'm afraid you've caught me at an awkward time.

PHOEBE

Yes, there's a hippopotamus in the room isn't there? It's an expression. There's something present that neither of us wants to acknowledge. But we both know it's there, don't we?

JASON

We do?

PHOEBE

I've been thinking about what you were doing when I came back in here just now.

JASON

Miss Craddock, I really don't think it's necessary to—

PHOEBE

No, I believe we should bring it out in the open. You were dancing around the room in a bizarre fashion and uttering odd, guttural sounds. Well, I want you to know that I don't think any the worse of you for that.

JASON

Thank you.

PHOEBE

Sometimes when I'm alone in the classroom I hook my feet over a rafter, hang upside down and sing "Night And Day." I mean we all do peculiar things when we're alone.

(Despite himself, he is touched by her kindness and starts to become intrigued by her)

JASON

You're very kind.

(Phoebe becomes uncomfortable under his gaze)

PHOEBE

I feel like an idiot. There's perspiration trickling down my back, and the strap on my slip has broken.

JASON

There's no need for you to have told me that.

PHOEBE

Bad habit.

JASON

What?

PHOEBE

Telling people before they notice it themselves. You know, "I'm

Phoebe Craddock, I have squinty eyes and I'm messy looking but I hope you like me anyway."

JASON

You said you've seen all my plays?

PHOEBE

Twenty-eight times.

JASON

Each?

PHOEBE

In Boston—when you were trying out. I put myself through school working as an usher at the Colonial Theater.

JASON

Ushers usually don't watch plays. They sit in the lobby and talk too loudly.

PHOEBE

Not me. I saw everything but I always liked the romantic comedies best. I mean I realize they weren't representative of the real world as we know it—at least as I know it—there isn't an abundance of elegance or wit where I was raised—I mean you could go a lifetime in my neighborhood without anyone saying anything you'd want to put in a play. Shut up, Phoebe.

JASON

I beg your pardon?

PHOEBE

I suppose I feel if I keep talking I won't have to hear what you have to say about my play.

JASON

I'm sorry. I haven't had time to really read it yet.

(There is a slight pause)

PHOEBE

May I sit for a moment?

JASON

Of course.

PHOEBE

Thank you. I feel a little faint. From *relief*. Isn't that silly?

JASON

(Gently)

No, I understand perfectly. It's no fun being naked.

PHOEBE

It's quite curious. Did you know one's knees actually do knock when one is apprehensive?

(He is staring at her)

Is there lipstick on my teeth?

JASON

What? Oh, no. I have this strange feeling we've met before.

PHOEBE

We have. It was about five years ago. You were trying out *Blue Is For Boys*. Between the Wednesday matinee and evening performance I was in the Union Oyster House. You came in and sat at the only empty table, which happened to be right next to mine. Well, naturally I was thrilled and in a burst of girlish impetuousness I turned and blurted out a stream of totally incoherent compliments about how much I admired your work. You were very nice, listened politely and said "thank you." Still trembling from the encounter I turned away. I was drinking hot chocolate—you know with those small marshmallows floating on top? I had just taken a gulp when you suddenly said, "And what do you do?" The hot chocolate went down the wrong way, I choked slightly, and as I looked at you, I realized I had small marshmallows shooting out of my nose. You looked at me for a moment and then, very gravely, you said, "You know, not many people can do that."

JASON

It seems that our meetings are not destined to go smoothly.

PHOEBE

Not at all the way the characters in your plays would meet.

JASON

Only because I didn't think of it.

(They smile at one another)

PHOEBE

Do you need any help?

JASON

In my career?

PHOEBE

With your cuff links.

JASON

Thank you.

(She crosses to him, bends over to thread the cuff links. Jason, conscious of her closeness, is staring at her. She looks up)

PHOEBE

I'm sorry, I'm all thumbs.
(She notices his stare)
What is it?

JASON

You don't smell musty.

PHOEBE

(At a loss)
Uh—thank you.

JASON

My ex-partner smelled musty.

PHOEBE

(Puzzled)
He wasn't that old was he?

JASON

No.

(She goes back to putting the cuff links in)

PHOEBE

I'm afraid I've crumpled your cuff.

(Jason is looking at her with an odd, incredulous expression. Disturbed and somewhat bewildered by his reaction to her, he abruptly picks up her script, flips it open)

JASON

Why did you want me to read your play?

PHOEBE

I stole the leading character from you.

(He looks up from the script)

JASON

Which one?

PHOEBE

The girl you used to write in the fifties. The high-spirited but basically "nice" girl who always faced the dilemma of whether to forfeit her virginity or hold onto it until the final curtain. You remember her?

JASON

Of course. Patti—Sally—Mary.

PHOEBE

(A thought hits her)
Why did they all have such short names?

JASON

They're easy to type.
(He goes back to reading script)

PHOEBE

Ah. Well, whatever happened to her?

JASON

She always successfully defended her virginity, married the leading man, moved to Scarsdale, had 2.7 children and lived happily ever after.

PHOEBE
(Nervously—very aware of him reading her script)
Exactly. But what if she didn't live happily ever after? Supposing twenty years later—today—she went through a divorce. Now in her late thirties, still attractive, she's suddenly single again and is plunged into an entirely new world with a whole new sexual morality. How does she cope with that?

JASON
The Girl In The Back Seat.

PHOEBE
Well, that's where most of us ended up fighting for our honor, isn't it?

(He looks at her)

JASON
What do you know about fifties' sexual mores? Aren't you part of the permissive sixties?

PHOEBE
No, I'm extremely backward. I mean in that way.

(He breaks eye contact, moves to window, reading script)

Anyway, I borrowed your character, added twenty years and took it from there.

JASON
You don't know how to construct a scene and your dialogue is stilted.

PHOEBE
You can tell all that from three pages?

JASON
(Testily)
Look, I do hope you're not going to be—*sensitive!*

PHOEBE
Why do you say my dialogue is stilted?

JASON

The girl says "purchase" instead of "buy," "obtain" instead of "get" and "plight" instead of "trouble." People don't talk like that.

PHOEBE

I do.

JASON

You're an English teacher from a small village in Vermont and I have the suspicion you're quite eccentric.

PHOEBE

Spotted that, did you?

JASON

You know that about yourself?

PHOEBE

No. I only said it because I didn't want to appear sensitive.

JASON

(Impatiently)

Look, when I said you were eccentric I meant it as a compliment!

PHOEBE

Thank you. I think you're eccentric too.

JASON

Why?

PHOEBE

You do peculiar things when you're alone.

JASON

So do you.

PHOEBE

No, I don't. I made that up to lessen your embarrassment.

JASON

Miss Craddock, you have a warped view of life.

PHOEBE

Another compliment?

JASON

Essential for someone who wants to write comedy. But it's only a start.

(She moves to collect her things)

PHOEBE

Yes, well, I certainly appreciate your taking the time to see me.

(She starts for the door)

JASON

Would you stop teaching and move to New York to work with me?

(She turns)

PHOEBE

I thought you hated my play?

JASON

Why would you think that?

PHOEBE

You said I didn't know how to construct a scene and my dialogue was stilted.

JASON

My dialogue is brilliant.

PHOEBE

You really want to work with me?

JASON

I'm not sure yet. Look, you'd better sit down.

(She does. His manner is still brusque)

Miss Craddock, what do you think the theatre is?

PHOEBE

A celebration of the human condition.

JASON

(Impatiently)

No, that's not what I'm talking about. Are you single?

PHOEBE

Yes.

JASON

Do you plan on getting married?

PHOEBE

Eventually.

JASON

That's not good enough.

PHOEBE

I didn't know this was an exam.

JASON

Look, I don't plan on us becoming Will and Ariel Durant. But I don't want to invest in a partnership and then have you suddenly get the urge to become a nursing mother.

PHOEBE

I see.

JASON

No, you don't. You don't know a damn thing about the theatre. The working conditions are intolerable, the people you have to deal with are egocentric maniacs, and it's filled with rejections on every level. When you're writing comedy the opposite of success is not failure—it's embarrassment. And it's very public. They write head-lines, Miss Craddock!
(He is unhappy with his knot, tears it apart and starts again)
All right, that's the pleasant part. You'll be working with me and I am a difficult person. In fact, some people think I am *impossible*. I am demanding, selfish, obsessive, moody, arrogant, rarely satisfied and my own mother once said I lack warmth. Would you be willing to accept those conditions?

PHOEBE

Sounds like a lot of fun.

JASON

All right, dammit, we'll give it a try!
(He angrily turns away again)

PHOEBE

I just have one question.

(He looks at her)

Why are you so *angry*?

(There is a pause)

JASON

(Finally—quietly)
Well, what do you expect? You barge in here unannounced, disrupt
my life, and then have the gall to be talented.

(She doesn't know what to say to this)

I'm sorry. It's—your timing. I'd made certain—plans.

(She is still puzzled)

(Evasively)
Also this damned tie won't tie.

PHOEBE

Maybe I can help.
(She moves to him, knots tie through following)
My mother died when I was young so I've been tying my father's
and three brothers' ties for years. I can cook, darn socks, even cut
hair if required.

JASON

(Conscious of her closeness)
A simple Windsor knot will do for now.

(She finishes knotting the tie, pats it in place)

PHOEBE

There.

(They are standing very close, both now aware of the current
between them)

JASON

(With a tone of quiet disbelief)
You're not my type at all you know.

(The moment is shattered as Allison St. James, in a bridal dress and veil, enters the room. She is a beautiful, friendly, young woman with an open, direct manner. She stops and surveys the two)

ALLISON

Fine state of affairs. Two minutes before our wedding I discover my fiancé with another woman.

JASON

(Flustered)
Allison, you shouldn't be here.

ALLISON

Oh, I don't believe in those old superstitions.
        (She moves to him, kisses him)
I just had to find out if you're as terrified as I am.
        (She slips her arm through his, smiles at the stunned Phoebe)
I don't believe we've met.

JASON

(Very flustered)
I'm sorry. Miss—
        (Goes blank on her name)
—uh—I'd like you to meet—uh—
        (He goes blank again)
My fiancée.

ALLISON

(Amused at his nervousness)
Allison. I didn't catch *your* name.

PHOEBE

Craddock—P.J.—Phoebe.

JASON

Miss Craddock—is going to be my new writing partner.

ALLISON

When did this happen?

JASON

What happen? Oh, just today.

ALLISON

That's marvelous! We'll have the same anniversary.

(They stare at her)

Your partnership and our marriage. We'll be able to all celebrate together.
(To Phoebe)
You're staying for the wedding I hope.

JASON

Her?

ALLISON

Darling, I know *you* are.
(To Phoebe)
I'll throw you the bouquet.

PHOEBE

I'm sorry—I'm from Vermont.

(Allison is puzzled)

JASON

It was Blanche's fault. She came a week early. And she's a woman.

ALLISON

(Not understanding)
That's—too bad.
(To Jason—playfully)
Well, sir—what do you think? Still want to go through with this thing?

JASON

Yes—well, I've had trouble tying my tie.
(He moves away to put on his jacket)

ALLISON

Jason, did you know you're not making any sense at all?

JASON

I'm not?

ALLISON

That's okay. You've made me feel better.

JASON

Oh?

ALLISON

You're obviously as terrified as I am.
 (She moves to door, turns)
I hope we'll be good friends, Phoebe.
 (To Jason)
As for you—I'll see you around, huh?
 (She blows him a kiss and exits)

PHOEBE

 (Finally)
She's very beautiful.

JASON

Yes.

PHOEBE

She seems nice.

JASON

She is, actually.

PHOEBE

Lively.

JASON

Very.

PHOEBE

She's obviously very fond of you. Well—naturally.

JASON

Hmm.

PHOEBE

Very flat, Norfolk.

 (He looks at her)

JASON

What?

PHOEBE

We were sounding very Noel Cowardish. It's a line from one of his plays.

JASON

Private Lives.

PHOEBE

First scene.

JASON

They met on their respective honeymoons, fell in love, and ran away together at the end of the first act.

. (A beat)

Marvelous.

PHOEBE

And he made it totally believable.

JASON

Anything's believable if it's done well.

(They look at one another for a moment)

Would you like a drink?

PHOEBE

(Gratefully)

Yes, I really would.

(He moves to pour two drinks)

JASON

Scotch?

PHOEBE

It doesn't matter. I don't drink.

(He turns to look at her)

It seems—fitting.

(Finally)
It's been quite a day.

JASON

Oh?

PHOEBE

Well, I meet my girlhood idol, he asks me to work with him; and then rushes off to get married.
(A beat)
Extraordinary.

JASON

Oh, I don't know. Boy meets girl, boy gets girl, boy loses girl. Been done a million times.
(They are gazing at one another as Blanche enters through the double doors)

BLANCHE

Places please. Let's get this show on the road.
(She stops as she sees Phoebe)
Who's she?

JASON

Long story. I'll explain later.

BLANCHE

Well, it's now or never, kid.

JASON

I'll be right there.

(Blanche exits. Jason holds his glass up in a toast. Finally)
Phoebe—to us.

(They both drink. He puts his glass down, moves to the double doors, opens them. We hear a low murmur from outside. He looks out the door. Slowly he turns and looks at Phoebe. They are in this position as the *CURTAIN FALLS*)

END OF SCENE 1

Scene 2

TIME: A year later. Very late at night.

AT RISE: It is raining outside. The stage is dark except for a
           small pool of light which emanates from an end table
           lamp and illuminates Jason who is sitting on the sofa,
           a folded New York *Times* beside him. He is wearing
           an overcoat and scarf and is steadily drinking from a
           large tumbler of Scotch, his face impassive. He shows
           no sign of drunkenness. Blanche, dressed in a fur coat
           over evening wear, appears in the doorway, regards
           him for a moment.

BLANCHE
Is getting drunk the answer?

JASON
No, but it makes you forget the question.

(She touches a light switch and some other lamps go on)

BLANCHE
The *audience* really loved it, Jason.

JASON
(A statement)
You saw the *Times* notice.

(She gives a little shrug, removes her fur coat, moves to de-
posit it)

BLANCHE

Listen, it'll do very well in stock. Why'd you leave the party so early?

JASON

My cheeks started to ache from smiling as if I didn't care. Felt like "Miss Rhode Island." How's Phoebe taking it?

BLANCHE

I don't know. She left right after that horrible thing she did.

JASON

What horrible thing?

(Blanche shudders slightly)

BLANCHE

It's too horrible to talk about. Be nice to her, Jason. She's probably feeling very fragile.

JASON

I don't exactly feel like a Mack truck myself.

(Phoebe enters. She is soaking wet and is wearing a raincoat, buttoned incorrectly, over an evening dress that has seen better days. She pauses inside the door, attempts a bright smile)

PHOEBE

Well, the theatre certainly is character building, isn't it?

(Jason has been looking at her appearance)

JASON

Jesus, who dresses you—Quasimodo? You okay?

PHOEBE

Well, I do have some questions.

JASON

The only answer for that is a drink.

PHOEBE

No, thank you. I believe I'm still quite "squiffed." Tonight I found out that I cannot drink.

JASON

Oh?

(Phoebe nods thoughtfully)

PHOEBE

I threw up on the mayor's shoes. Well, *in* the mayor's shoes. Shoe.
(She gives up on the wet buttons)
His right shoe.

(Jason moves to her, unbuttons her coat, attempts to get her
out of it as one would undress a child)

JASON

How did you manage that?

PHOEBE

He was sitting next to me at the party. He'd taken off his right shoe.
I'd had two banana daiquiris. I must say he was very nice about it.

JASON

Well, he's always been a big supporter of the Arts.
(To Blanche)
Was that the horrible thing she did?

BLANCHE

No, that was later.

PHOEBE

Would you mind if I didn't talk about that for a few years?

(Jason moves to help her out of her raincoat. He hands her
purse and rain hat to Blanche)

JASON

Pull your arm out of this—no, the other arm—look, just stand still
and don't do anything—that's it.
(He gets the coat off, hands it to Blanche, who takes it to
the library steps)
Go and sit over there.
(He indicates the sofa. Phoebe crosses to sit while Jason gets
a lap robe from the ottoman in front of the wing chair. He
crosses with it to Phoebe. Nervously—)

You're not going to throw up again, are you?

> (He puts the blanket around Phoebe's shoulders. He kneels
> to take off her wet shoes)

PHOEBE

No, I was just wondering why I feel like a criminal. I mean we
didn't commit an actual crime, did we?

JASON

Just a misdemeanor.

PHOEBE

Then why do I feel like Lizzie Borden? Is that normal?

JASON

Oh, I think it's fairly natural. After all, the murder weapon's in full
view at the Booth Theatre. Blanche, I think this girl could use some
coffee. Would you tell the cook to make some?

> (Blanche has been watching him curiously)

What's the matter?

BLANCHE

She's very good for you, Jason. Brings out your better nature.
> (She exits)

JASON

Don't take it too hard, kid—it's only a play. In fifty years' time only
you and I will remember. And I'm not too sure about "I."

> (He crosses to the bar to make a drink)

PHOEBE

It's not only the play. It's what I did at the party in front of all
those people.

JASON

Well, since it seems to be in the public domain, maybe you should
tell me about it.

PHOEBE

> (In dull voice)

There was a great deal of noise and confusion. Then someone

rushed in the door with a newspaper in his hand. He shoved it at me and said, "It's marvelous—it's all about you!" I scrambled up on top of a table and yelled, "Quiet everyone—I have a wonderful review from the *Times!*"
(A beat)
Now you may be wondering why I did that.

JASON
It does seem somewhat uncharacteristic.

PHOEBE
My only excuse is that I was—overstimulated. Of course everyone immediately became silent and I began to read the review in my best, loud, clear, schoolteacher voice. Well, it was an absolutely horrendous notice. All the people were staring up at me as if I was—
(She searches for the right word)
—demented. It was—horrible. I tried skipping paragraphs—editing out the bad parts, but it was difficult because—I'm somewhat astigmatic—and there were no *good* parts. Gradually this confused—babble—filled the room and—I'm having trouble concentrating—I'd like to stop talking now.

JASON
Who was the son of a bitch who gave you the paper?

PHOEBE
My father. Oh, it wasn't his fault. He thought it was exciting just to be *mentioned*.
(She looks at him)
Was it as humiliating as I think it was?

JASON
You feeling better now?

PHOEBE
Sleepy. Incredibly sleepy. Do you think that's the alcohol?

JASON
Either that or the bananas.
(He sits beside her on the sofa)
Why don't you put your head down?

(Much to his surprise, she doesn't lean the other way but gratefully puts her head on his lap and closes her eyes)

You'll be okay, kid. Oh, for a few days you'll be a little gun shy. You'll be afraid to open menus in restaurants in case there's a bad review there—but eventually the pain will go away and be replaced by something much easier to live with—bitterness.

PHOEBE

(Sleepily)
You're trying to make me laugh.

JASON

Not too successfully, it seems.

PHOEBE

But I appreciate—the thought.
(She seems to have drifted off to sleep.

He gently strokes her hair)

JASON

Sweet dreams, kid.

(At this point Allison enters. Still beautiful, tastefully dressed, she seems somewhat more cheerful than the occasion demands and we sense an underlying tension between her and Jason. She stops as she sees Jason and Phoebe)

ALLISON

(Finally)
Do you ever get the feeling we're drifting apart?

(Jason turns to look at her but continues to absently stroke Phoebe's hair)

JASON

Just comforting a comrade wounded in the field of battle.

ALLISON

That's weird. I mean usually she's so shy around you.
(She takes off her coat and deposits it)

JASON

I think it's the liquor talking.

(Allison sits down on the other end of the sofa, takes Phoebe's feet in her lap)

ALLISON

Her feet are freezing, poor dear.
(She warms her feet with her hands during the following)
I'm sorry about the play.

JASON

You mean the notices?

ALLISON

Are they that important?

JASON

Only if you want people to buy tickets.

ALLISON

Don't patronize me, Jason. I may not know anything about the theatre but I'm not an idiot.

JASON

It's all right, Allison. I know you never liked the play.

ALLISON

It's not that I didn't like it. It's just that I didn't think it was *about* anything.

JASON

(Wearily)
It was about giving an audience an entertaining evening.
(Allison looks down at Phoebe)

ALLISON

Was it that hard on her?

JASON

Allison, we just saw a year's work go down the drain. She's given up a career, spent all her savings and tonight it all blew up in her face.
(A beat)
And how was *your* day?

ALLISON

What are you going to do?

JASON

Have an affair or buy a new hat. I'll think of something.

(She regards him for a moment)

ALLISON

Jason, we need to talk.

JASON

I thought we were.

ALLISON

I mean about us.

JASON

(Finally)
Does it have to be tonight?

ALLISON

Yes. I have something important to tell you. I've been waiting until
after you got the play open.
(She gets up, moves away)
It didn't seem fair to burden you with it before.

JASON

Suddenly I'm cold sober.

ALLISON

Well, I think we should be alone for this sort of discussion.

JASON

Then why did you bring it up now?

ALLISON

(A trifle tartly)
I just wanted you to pencil it in on your appointment pad.

(They are looking at one another as Blanche, carrying a tray
containing coffee, enters)

BLANCHE

Sorry I was so long. I was on the phone to Harry, trying to get some
word on the other reviews.

JASON

And?

BLANCHE

I guess they weren't in the mood for charm, Jason.

(There is a gloomy pause)

ALLISON

(Finally)

So—is it okay if I get out of my "lucky" dress now?

(Blanche and Jason both turn to look at her)

Sorry. I was just trying to lighten the situation.

BLANCHE

You want some coffee?

ALLISON

No thanks, Blanche. I really do need to get out of these clothes.

(She moves to door, turns)

I think Phoebe might feel better if she stayed with us tonight. I'll bring her some blankets and she can bunk down in your dressing room.

(Allison exits. Blanche pours coffee through following)

BLANCHE

She's sweet.

JASON

She's a snob.

BLANCHE

(Surprised)

Allison's the least snobbish person I know.

JASON

I mean about the theatre.

BLANCHE

Well, you're a snob about everything *but* the theatre.

(At this point Phoebe sits bolt upright)

PHOEBE

Oh, my God!
> (She stands up, looking very disoriented. Jason and Blanche
> have also jumped up)

BLANCHE

What is it?

PHOEBE

I—I had this terrible dream. I was at this opening night party and
someone shoved a newspaper in my hand and—
> (As the realization hits her)
Oh, my God.

JASON

I think she's still "squiffed."

> (Blanche hands Phoebe a cup of coffee)

BLANCHE

Here, drink this.

JASON

I'd better change. My lap feels a little warm and damp.

PHOEBE
> (Embarrassed)
I'm terribly sorry.

JASON

That's all right. It felt quite agreeable.
> (He exits to the dressing room)

PHOEBE

Did I pass out?

BLANCHE

No, you just went to sleep in Jason's lap.

PHOEBE
> (Stunned)
I actually went to sleep in his *lap*?

> (Blanche nods)

What did he do?

BLANCHE

He stroked your hair.

PHOEBE

He stroked my *hair?*
    (Blanche nods)

PHOEBE

How—odd. I mean, Jason is not a physical person. We rarely touch.

BLANCHE

Well, you touched tonight.

PHOEBE

And I missed it.
    (She sips coffee for a moment)
Do you know I never call him anything?

BLANCHE

    (Puzzled)
What?

PHOEBE

Well, it seemed silly to call him Mr. Carmichael and although he asked me to call him Jason, I could never quite bring myself to do that.

BLANCHE

That must have made things a bit difficult when you were working together.

PHOEBE

Yes. I always had to wait until he looked at me before I could talk. Will they close the play tomorrow?

BLANCHE

Nothing lasts forever, kid. What are you going to do?

PHOEBE

Go back to the classroom, I suppose.
    (A small shrug)
It's probably all for the best.

BLANCHE

I know what you mean.

PHOEBE
(Flustered)
Is the way I feel about him that obvious?

BLANCHE
(Gently)
Only to the trained eye. Get a good night's sleep, honey. We'll talk tomorrow.
(Blanche crosses to get her coat)
Oh, Jason . . . Jason, I'm leaving. I'll see you in the morning at the funeral arrangements.
(She exits. Jason, wearing a dressing gown over his dinner shirt and trousers, enters. He crosses to close the door behind Blanche)

JASON
Look, would it be all right with you if I dropped the arrogant facade, got sloppy drunk and whined and sniveled a lot?

PHOEBE
I'd consider that a privilege.

(They look at one another for a moment)

JASON
Do me a favor, Phoebe—don't.

PHOEBE
Don't what?

JASON
Don't make a speech.

PHOEBE
How did you know I was going to make a speech?

(He moves to pour himself a drink)

JASON
Your eyes start to water and you get an odd, pinched look around the bridge of your nose.
(He turns to face her)
Anyway, it's my turn.

PHOEBE

(Surprised)
Your turn?

JASON

Yes.

(He paces for a moment, turns to face her)
Phoebe—don't let them get to you.

(She waits but there is no more)

PHOEBE

(Incredulous)
That's it? "Don't let them get to me?"

JASON

That's about it. I know this whole experience must have been
difficult for you but—

PHOEBE

(Emotionally)
Difficult? The first week of rehearsal I was bitten by a rat! The second week I was mugged in the elevator—and then in Philadelphia I
became quite unhinged and almost tackled a middle-aged woman
around the knees to prevent her from leaving the theatre. After forc-
ing her into a seat and hissing, "You'll miss the best part!" I discovered she was one of the ushers. This whole experience was capped
tonight when I regurgitated into the shoe of a public official, stood
up on a table to happily announce my inadequacies to a crowd of
total strangers, fell asleep in your lap and dribbled on your overcoat,
and—

(Her eyes welling up)
—it was the best time I've had in my entire life!!

JASON

Then why are you crying?

PHOEBE

(Tearfully)
Because it's all over!

(Very touched, Jason sits next to her and puts his arm around her so that her head rests on his shoulder.

Finally)
I'm wetting you again.

JASON

(Brusquely; moving away)
Yes, and it's something that should be nipped firmly in the bud. Now, if you promise to stop, I'll promise to be better next time.

PHOEBE

(Stunned)
Next time?

JASON

On the next play.

PHOEBE

You mean you want to go on working with me?

JASON

You think I'm going to take the rap alone?

PHOEBE

But—but I don't understand. Everyone said this play didn't have the quality of your others because of me.

JASON

They were right.

(She stares at him)

You let me take your play, remove all the charm and sentiment and substitute jokes. If we're going to keep working together, you've got to stop letting me bully you. You're my partner, not my student, so at least once a month I suggest you tell me I'm a horse's ass. Look, if you're even *thinking* of making a speech, I'll withdraw the offer.

PHOEBE

It's not a speech. I just don't want you to do this out of loyalty—or misplaced compassion. I realize my behavior tonight has been rather —erratic, but, actually, I'm quite resilient. I'll survive.

JASON

Well, I'm not sure I will.

(As she looks at him: Awkwardly)
The reason I'm asking you to stay is not *only* professional. I've—I've grown—attached to you.

(Her gaze disconcerts him, causing him to blurt)
Phoebe, Allison and I are separating.

PHOEBE

(Absolutely stunned)
When did this happen?

JASON

It's still only a rumor, but, as you know, bad rumors generally turn out to be true.
(Embarrassed)
Look, I feel uncomfortable talking about this. The point is I'm going to need a friend.

PHOEBE

(Sympathetically)
Is there anything I can do?

JASON

(Gently)
Yes—go wash your face. When you come back we'll both get really drunk and convince each other that none of this is our fault.
(She moves to the dressing room door, turns, has difficulty saying his name but finally manages it)

PHOEBE

Jason?

JASON

Oh, God, you're really going to do it, aren't you?

PHOEBE

(Rather formally)
Jason, I know how any display of emotion embarrasses you, but that's all the more reason why this must be said. I—I needed someone tonight and I want to thank you for letting me be your friend.

(She quickly exits to the dressing room.

Allison, wearing a dressing gown, and carrying some blankets, enters)

ALLISON

Well, has my pal sobered up yet?

JASON

I wasn't drunk—just shell shocked.

ALLISON

I meant Phoebe.
    (She puts blanket down, starts to leave but at the door turns and stops)
I've thought of a hundred ways to tell you this but—well, I suppose the best way is to keep it simple.

JASON

    (Warily)
Always.

ALLISON

The trouble is, it's not that simple.
    (She sits)
You know, when I married you I really didn't know what I was getting into. Because of the—well, the sort of plays you write I suppose I assumed you just spend a couple of hours every morning dashing them off. It takes a lot longer than that, doesn't it?

JASON

    (A trifle bitterly)
Yes, it takes a lot of thought to appear glib.

ALLISON

Please, Jason. Anyway, I decided I needed to find something to fill my time. Then a few weeks ago the solution presented itself. Jason, I'm pregnant.

JASON

    (Dumbfounded)
Pregnant?

ALLISON

Two months. I put off telling you because I knew you were preoccupied and—
        (She gives a small shrug)
—I thought if the play was a success we could have a double celebration. Now—well, would you accept it as a consolation prize?
        (He is still staring at her.

        She gives a little laugh)
Hey, I expected surprise but not catatonia.

JASON

I'm sorry. I'm very happy.

ALLISON

You *look* as if you've just lost your best friend.

        (This innocent remark is not lost on him)

JASON

It's fatigue.

ALLISON

Maybe I shouldn't have hit you with it tonight.

JASON

No, it's—it's nice to know something I collaborated on turned out right.
        (He moves to her)
Really, I'm very pleased.

        (They embrace for a moment. She looks at him)

ALLISON

Are we going to be all right, Jason?

JASON

        (Finally)
Sure—we'll run for years.

ALLISON

You looked exhausted. Come to bed.

JASON

I'll—I'll be right up.

(Allison exits.

Phoebe, her face scrubbed clean, enters)

PHOEBE

Did you know you're the only person I know who has mono-grammed soap?

JASON

(Distracted)

What? Oh, when I'm not wearing clothes I'm not sure who I am.

(She notices his expression)

PHOEBE

Are you all right?

JASON

I'm fine.

(Briskly)

Look, tomorrow's going to be rather hectic so let's plan on a work session at ten a.m. on Friday, okay?

(Very confused, she manages a nod)

Good night, Phoebe.

(He exits.

Totally bewildered, Phoebe tries to fathom what has just taken place. She does this by miming what happened *before* she left the room and then what happened *after* she came back. It doesn't help and she stands in the middle of the room, completely baffled.

Jason reappears in the doorway)

JASON

Oh, I think you should know that Allison—well, she got pregnant.

PHOEBE

While I was out of the room? I'm sorry, I'm still a little—scattered.

(Jason turns to exit, turns back)

JASON

(Awkwardly)

Uh—if I were you—I'd pray for a girl.

PHOEBE

Why?

JASON

I'd like to name her after you.

PHOEBE

Me?

JASON

Didn't I ever tell you? I've always liked the name Phoebe.

(They look at one another for a brief moment before he exits quickly.

Phoebe slowly moves to the coffee table, picks up the brandy snifter and tosses all the brandy down as the *CURTAIN FALLS*)

END OF ACT ONE

ACT TWO

Scene 1

TIME: Ten years later. A November morning in 1976.

AT RISE: Jason, now in his mid-forties, looking elegant in casual, expensive "work clothes," is sitting on the sofa reading some loose typewritten pages.

               Phoebe, now in her mid-thirties, wearing a shapeless, worn jogging suit and an old baseball cap, is sitting with a sewing basket beside her, patching the knees of a child's jeans.

               Jason looks up from the pages, looks off into space, frowning.

PHOEBE

Well?

JASON

    (Vaguely)
It's fine.

PHOEBE

Jason, I worked six hours rewriting that scene!

    (He tosses the pages aside onto the coffee table)

JASON

I said it was fine.

PHOEBE

You always say that when you mean "okay," "not good enough,"
"less than wonderful."

(He starts to pace)

JASON

(Frustrated)
It's not the scene. The scene's fine. It's the whole damned second
act.

PHOEBE

So we'll change it.

JASON

I don't know, it seems like rearranging the deck chairs on the Ti-
tanic.
(He looks at her; irritably)
Why do you wear that hat?

PHOEBE

It keeps my hair in place when I'm jogging.

JASON

It makes you look like—

PHOEBE

Katharine Hepburn.

JASON

Yogi Berra.

PHOEBE

Yes, everyone says that. What we need is—

JASON

A good rationale for him remaining faithful to his wife.

PHOEBE

All right. He loves her.

JASON

I mean something the audience will buy.
(He sighs, shakes his head)

It used to be so much easier. You had a boy and girl and then you took three acts to dream them into bed together.

PHOEBE

I *still* like that story.

JASON

I mean, we must be insane! Half the world out there is doing obscene things to the other half and we're writing a play about a man who's *thinking* of cheating on his wife.

PHOEBE

People still respond to Romantic Comedies, Jason. You just have to write them differently.

JASON

(Suddenly)

Tell me something. Why did they take the running boards off cars?

PHOEBE

I give up.

JASON

Why did they take the elegance out of everything? Everything used to be better. Food, trains, cars, newspapers, music, hotels, movies, clothes. Everything.

(A beat)

Maybe it's me. Maybe *I* was better.

PHOEBE

Are you depressed just because of the play?

(He looks at her)

JASON

Do you ever get the feeling you're living out of your times?

PHOEBE

Yes—but then I always have. Until last Thursday I wanted to be Jane Austen.

(They are both lost in thought. Phoebe with her clipboard in hand is absently wandering and making a sucking noise with her teeth)

JASON

I really wish you wouldn't do that.

PHOEBE

Do what?

JASON

Suck your teeth.

PHOEBE

I'm trying to think of a reason for the husband's fidelity.

JASON

So am I, but your oral hygiene isn't helping much.

(She nods thoughtfully and then suddenly falls to the floor onto her hands and goes into a series of vigorous push-ups.

He absently gazes at her rear end going up and down. The double doors open and Allison enters. Thirty years old, she wears a minimum of makeup with a simple hairstyle which, combined with her understated, tailored clothes, gives her the look of an attractive, capable businesswoman. Jason looks up)

Allison, can't you see we're working?

ALLISON

(Waving a report card in her hand)

I'm sorry, darling. I just had to tell Phoebe about Timmy's report card.

(Allison crosses to Phoebe and hands her the report card)

PHOEBE

Oh, this is marvelous! I knew he could do it!

ALLISON

Well, you're the one who deserves the gold star.

(To Jason)

Do you realize how many hours she spent tutoring Timmy? Thanks, Phoebe.

PHOEBE

Well—I like to keep my hand in. I'd better congratulate him, Where is he?

ALLISON

Outside—waiting to be congratulated.

PHOEBE

That's my boy!
>(She exits. Allison watches her go as Jason picks up the loose
>pages, studies them)

ALLISON

Sometimes I worry about her.

JASON

Why?

ALLISON
>(Sitting on the arm of sofa)
Oh, I don't know. She doesn't seem to have much of a life.

JASON

She's one of the most successful writers in America and, since she's
easily the cheapest, she's also one of the richest.
>(He goes back to studying the pages)
I should have her life.

ALLISON
>(Curiously)
What does she do about sex?

>(Jason looks up, surprised)

JASON

I have no idea.

ALLISON

Don't you ever ask her?

JASON

Allison, we work in here—we don't have pajama parties.

ALLISON

Oh, I know I hear a lot about the "anguish of creation," but I also
hear a lot of laughter coming out of this room.

>(He regards her with some surprise)

JASON

Are you *jealous* of Phoebe?

ALLISON

Yes, I suppose I am. I'm jealous of the ongoing love affair you two have with the theatre.

(A small shrug)

It's an obsession I can't share.

JASON

I could say that about your career in politics.

ALLISON

Oh, I'm not complaining, just stating a fact. Anyway, I just think she should be married.

JASON

(Shrugs)

That's her choice.

ALLISON

Not really. She's very influenced by you.

(He looks at her)

JASON

I *never* interfere with Phoebe's personal life.

ALLISON

Oh, come on, Jason. When that nice older man from Florida was taking her out, you said, "In five years he'll be walking around with his fly zipper not quite pulled up." That killed *that* romance.

JASON

It was just a passing observation.

ALLISON

No, you always seem able to come up with the perfect phrase to effectively eliminate anyone who gets even slightly interested in her.

JASON

What the hell are you driving at, Allison?

ALLISON

(Evenly)

Let her go, Jason.

(He looks at her for a moment)

JASON

Why are we talking about Phoebe?

ALLISON

Because it keeps us from talking about us, I suppose.

(They are looking at one another as Phoebe enters)

PHOEBE

Sorry I took so long. Kate Mallory phoned. She's in town doing some P.R. for her latest movie and wants to meet with us to—quote —conceptualize the thematic problems of the play—unquote.

ALLISON

Does she really talk like that?

JASON

(Glumly)

She's one of those people who uses the word "artist" a lot.

ALLISON

What's she like?

PHOEBE

Well, she's a curious combination.

JASON

Mean and dumb.

PHOEBE

So how are things at City Hall?

ALLISON

Well, I wouldn't buy any municipal bonds right now.
(Checking watch)
Which reminds me, I have a budget meeting in half an hour.
(She moves to door)
Thanks again, Phoebe. Every working mother should have a friend like you.
(She exits. Jason shakes his head)

JASON

I married Grace Kelly and I ended up with Bella Abzug.

PHOEBE

She's a bright woman, Jason. She needed more intellectual stimulation than writing out place settings.

(He looks up from script, regards her for a moment)

JASON

You really *like* her, don't you?

PHOEBE

Don't you?

JASON

I have to. She's my wife.

PHOEBE

You never cheat on her.

JASON

How do you know?

PHOEBE

Because when you're not with her, you're with me. Why don't you?

JASON

I'm not allowed. I believe it's one of the most important rules.

PHOEBE

That's not good enough, Jason.

JASON

I hate it when you lapse back into schoolmarmishness.

(She doesn't say anything)

All right. A few years ago I owned a delicate China teapot. One day I dropped it and it split right down the middle. Well, I glued it together and it looked as if it had never been broken. Then a few months later, for no apparent reason, it suddenly exploded into a thousand pieces. I suppose what I'm trying to say is that, despite all appearances, it's better to keep your teapot intact.

(Phoebe, furiously writing what Jason has been saying, crosses back to her chair stage right. When she is finished writing . . .)

PHOEBE

That's sweet.

JASON

Yes, I thought you'd buy that.

> (Phoebe puts her clipboard down and picks up a small cassette recorder and starts it. We hear the strains of "But Not For Me" played in a lush instrumental version)

Do you have to play that music?

PHOEBE

> (Absently)

It's the perfect mood music for writing this play.

JASON

But you've been playing it for six months now. I mean it's really getting on my nerves.

PHOEBE

What makes the husband suddenly fall in love with his wife again?

JASON

> (Muttering)

Pity we can't use the Cinderella convention.

PHOEBE

You mean where the girl takes off her glasses, lets down her hair and he realizes she's beautiful.

JASON

Don't laugh. Audiences used to love it.

PHOEBE

You think someone can fall in love that fast.

JASON

Of course. Even happened to me once.

> (Surprised, she looks at him)

It was at the Tony Awards a couple of years ago. I saw this woman from the back. She was wearing a blue taffeta dress and had gleaming blonde hair that cascaded down over creamy white shoulders. I fell instantly in love and remained that way for about five seconds.

(A shrug—casually)

Then she turned around and it was you.

PHOEBE

(Flustered)

Yes—well—you're right. I mean, I don't believe we can get away with Pygmalion anymore.

(We hear the front doorbell ring)

JASON

Who the hell can that be?

PHOEBE

Probably Leo Janowitz.

JASON

My God, he's been hanging around for three weeks. Doesn't he have a story by now?

PHOEBE

I thought you found him amusing.

JASON

That doesn't mean I want to adopt him.

PHOEBE

It was green actually.

JASON

Green?

PHOEBE

The dress. It was from the second scene of *Somewhere Every Summer*. I borrowed it from wardrobe.

JASON

I might have known you wouldn't have bought it.

(The door opens and Leo Janowitz enters. In his mid-thirties, has unruly hair, is dressed in a rumpled suit, and has a serious, reserved demeanor that almost masks a very dry sense of humor. His speech has the rough edges of the street and he tends to cut through to the core of things. He carries a small notebook and pencil)

LEO
(Without preamble—checking notes)
I know you're busy but I just wanted to check some facts. What year did you graduate from Yale?

JASON
Look, I'd prefer that you didn't mention I went to Yale.

LEO
Bad school?

JASON
I don't like anything published about my background that could cause people to pigeonhole me.

LEO
I don't get it.

PHOEBE
I think Jason means he would rather be judged by his work alone.

LEO
Yeah?

JASON
Have you seen any of my plays?

LEO
Nope. Read 'em all.

(Jason waits for the compliment. There is only a pause)

JASON
Look, there's one thing you should know—I'm not offended by flattery.

LEO
I don't know anything about the theatre.

JASON
Then why were you given this piece to write?

LEO

It's a fill-in assignment until I can get back to my serious stuff.

PHOEBE

(Quickly)
Leo just got back from two years in Russia.

JASON

You're an expert on Russia?

LEO

Yeah—well, I speak the lingo.

JASON

How many other "lingoes" do you speak?

LEO

A few.

JASON

You mind if *I* ask a question?

(Leo shrugs)

I suspect that underneath that unkempt exterior you're an educated, civilized man. Why do you go to all that trouble to hide it with bad tailoring?

LEO

It's no trouble.

JASON

(Moving to door)
Is that all?

LEO

Just one more thing.
(Checking notebook)
What's your biggest regret?

JASON

That Americans can't be knighted.
(He exits)

LEO

Miss Craddock?

PHOEBE

(Crossing to him)

Yes?

(Leo grabs her and kisses her)

Please, Leo—Jason could come back in.

LEO

So? He's not your father.

PHOEBE

(Moving away)

Well, he is in a way.

LEO

Professionally?

PHOEBE

Every way. A writing collaboration is a very intimate relationship.

LEO

Yeah, I been meaning to ask you about that.

(She looks at him)

PHOEBE

This for the article?

LEO

I've already written the article. I wanted an excuse to see you.

PHOEBE

Why?

LEO

I got the hots for you.

PHOEBE

(Flustered)

Yes—well, I'm sorry you caught us at such a busy time.

LEO

Is it just that you've never learned to accept a compliment or do you really believe as a woman you're the pits? Every time I get personal, you change the subject.

PHOEBE

I'm sorry.
(Blushing)
I'm just not used to such—an overt response to my—girlish charms.

LEO

I want you to marry me, Phoebe.

(She stares at him)

PHOEBE

Are you serious?

LEO

Yes.
(She stares at him blankly)

What's the matter? Am I being too overt?

PHOEBE

(Sitting)
No, I—I just need a moment to absorb this.

LEO

Okay.
(He waits)
Absorbed it yet?

(She manages a nod)
So about Jason. You been to bed with him?

PHOEBE

Why—why would you even think that?

LEO

I'm a pragmatist. You're out of town together. It's an old axiom—desire plus opportunity usually equals humpage. Am I being too personal?

PHOEBE

Yes—you are.

LEO

There's a reason. I've been assigned to the Paris bureau. I leave in five weeks and I want to take you with me. The point is, I can't stick around until the third act to see who gets the girl.

PHOEBE

I see.

LEO

So—you have sex together?

PHOEBE

Once. Well, not together.

LEO

(Finally)
That's some trick.

PHOEBE

(Embarrassed)
I mean it was once for me. None for Jason—

(He is staring at her)

It's hard to explain. We were out of town with a show—in Chicago —and the play wasn't working—it never did work—we still don't know why. Anyway, we'd rewritten half the script, but it hadn't helped at all and we just didn't know how to fix it. One night we got back to the hotel, exhausted, our brains numb—totally depressed. We started to drink and Jason became quite drunk—and then—more out of frustration, I suppose—I don't know—he started to—to make love to me, but—right in the middle—he passed out.

LEO

In the middle?

PHOEBE

Well, if we're going to be technical, a third of the way through. It could have been a quarter. I'm only guessing, of course—I mean I have no means of comparison—with Jason, that is.

(She clears her throat)
When I woke up, he was gone.

LEO

Then what happened?

PHOEBE

That's it.

LEO

You never discussed it?

PHOEBE

Jason obviously didn't remember—or if he did—he didn't want to.

LEO

Are you in love with him, Phoebe?

PHOEBE

I was.

LEO

And now?

PHOEBE

Now we just write plays together.

LEO

So will you marry me?
(He holds up his hand)
Before you say anything you should know there are three answers.

PHOEBE

Three?

LEO

"Yes"—"No"—or "Let's talk about it some more."
(As she opens her mouth to speak)
But first—something to help you make up your mind. I love you,
Phoebe.
(He kisses her.

Jason enters now attired in an elegant suit. He stops, completely stunned by what he sees. After a moment, sensing

that someone else is in the room, Phoebe and Leo break apart. Phoebe is very embarrassed but Leo is totally unflustered and casually notes Jason's new wardrobe)

You look as if you're going somewhere important.

JASON

I am. My tailor's.
(He moves to desk, busies himself with some papers)
But we have to finish up some work first.

LEO

(Pleasantly)
Okay, I don't have to be hit by a truck.
(To Phoebe)
I'll be in touch, huh?

(She manages a nod and Leo exits. Jason is still making a great show of studying the script pages)

PHOEBE

(Finally)
You don't really want to work, do you?

JASON

Why do you say that?

PHOEBE

You never like to sit down and get creases before you visit your tailor.

JASON

(Still studying script—overly casual)
Do you mind telling me why he was doing that?

PHOEBE

He finds me attractive.

JASON

Oh, come on, Phoebe! You expect me to buy that?

(She can't think of a reply to this)

I mean, you must have done something to bring it on.

PHOEBE

You make it sound like a migraine headache.

JASON

(Impatiently)

You are trying to tell me that the first time he's left alone with you, he's overcome with desire and leaps on you?

PHOEBE

Of course not. We've been—seeing each other.

JASON

He's been interviewing you at night?

PHOEBE

No, it wasn't a professional thing. They were more—do they still call them "dates"?

JASON

(Sitting)

This is no time to be coy!

PHOEBE

(Puzzled)

Why are you so upset?

JASON

(Thrown)

Upset?

PHOEBE

You just sat down and creased yourself.

JASON

Well, naturally, I'm somewhat alarmed.

PHOEBE

Why?

JASON

(On his feet again)

You know, for someone so talented you can be remarkably obtuse! Don't you know anything?

PHOEBE

Now you're shouting.

JASON

Because you should know better! He's a *journalist!* He's a person who makes a living writing down what people say when they're off guard.

PHOEBE

We didn't discuss my work. We just—hung out together.

JASON

Hung out? Aren't you getting a little old for that sort of thing?

PHOEBE

I wish I could think of an answer to that, but right now I'm in the middle of a hot flash.

JASON

Are you trying to tell me this is a *romantic* relationship?

PHOEBE

I'm not trying to tell you anything. Jason, what is the *matter* with you?

JASON

I don't want to see you get hurt and depressed.

PHOEBE

Oh?

JASON

Yes, you know how difficult it is for you to be funny when you're depressed.

PHOEBE

I don't have any illusions about the way Leo feels about me.

(He looks at her, relaxes somewhat)

JASON

Good.

PHOEBE
(Rather enjoying herself)
He wants to marry me.

(Jason is absolutely floored)

JASON
(Finally)
How do you know?

PHOEBE
He asked me.

JASON
When?

PHOEBE
Just now.

JASON
(Incredulous)
While you were wearing that hat?

PHOEBE
Maybe he's a Yogi Berra fan.

JASON
I want you to stop seeing him.

PHOEBE
Why?

(He looks at her)

JASON
Do I really have to say it? You want me to spell it out for you?

PHOEBE
(Finally)
I'm not sure.

JASON
(Avoiding her eyes)
No, perhaps it *is* time we stopped skirting the issue. We're going to

have to deal with it sometime. Better now than when it's too late.

(He looks at her, takes a breath)
Phoebe, our second act doesn't work at all!

(Phoebe just stares at him, turns and exits.

Looking stage right at Phoebe's chair)
Leo's the sort of man who wears his bowling shirt when he's not bowling. He's a lot like Jimmy Breslin—but without the polish. If they made triple-knit suits, Leo would wear them.

(The *CURTAIN FALLS*)

END OF SCENE 1

Scene 2

TIME: Late afternoon, six weeks later.

AT RISE: The stage is empty. The double doors open and Blanche and Phoebe enter. They take off their coats and other winter paraphernalia during following.

PHOEBE

I hope nothing's happened to him.

BLANCHE

It's not like Jason not to keep an appointment. When was the last time you saw him?

PHOEBE

About two o'clock. He stormed out of rehearsals when the actors started improvising.

BLANCHE

Maybe he went to beat up on Lee Strasberg.

(Phoebe moves to dressing room entrance)

PHOEBE

(Calling)

Jason! Jason, are you here?

(There is a slight pause)

JASON

(Offstage)
Yes, what is it?

PHOEBE

Are you all right?

JASON

(Offstage)
Of course. I'll—I'll be right out.

(Phoebe and Blanche take off their coats)

BLANCHE

How are rehearsals going?

PHOEBE

Well, the leading man's a bit wooden.

BLANCHE

A bit wooden? The man's a talking tree! What else?

PHOEBE

Jason and Kate Mallory loathe each other.

BLANCHE

I'm on his side.

PHOEBE

Oh, I know she's impossible, but I really do think he's overreacting.

BLANCHE

What changes does she want?

PHOEBE

The same one. Beware of people with few ideas, Blanche. They cling to them with such tenacity.

BLANCHE

She still wants you to rewrite the ending?

PHOEBE

She doesn't want her character to go back to her husband. She's got this idea in her head that she's the Joan of Arc of the seventies and keeps saying, "Why should I end up with any man? Why can't I go off and make a life of my own?"

BLANCHE
How about you, my love? You look harassed.

PHOEBE
That's funny. I *feel* suicidal.

BLANCHE
Are you going to marry that nice young man?

PHOEBE
Well, I've gone from "no" to "perhaps"—but I'm not fooling anybody—not even me.

BLANCHE
Isn't he leaving for Paris in a couple of days?

PHOEBE
Oh, it's impossible, Blanche! Even if I wanted to get married, I can't walk out on Jason now.

BLANCHE
He'd survive.

(Surprised, Phoebe turns to look at her)
Oh, he'd scream bloody murder, but he'd survive.

PHOEBE
I take it this is my friend not my agent talking.

BLANCHE
(Shrugs)
I'd just hate to see you turn into one of those dotty women writers who drink too much and wear hats.

(Jason enters from his dressing room and crosses directly to his desk)

JASON
Pour me a double, will you, Blanche?

BLANCHE
Have you been eavesdropping?

JASON

Of course not. Who can hear anything over the clash of your brace-
lets?

BLANCHE

What are you doing back here anyway? You were supposed to meet
us at Sardi's.

JASON

Yes—well, something came up.

(At this point, Kate Mallory enters from the dressing room.

She is a soft, pretty woman in her late thirties with a decep-
tively gentle, feminine manner and sweet smile. She has absolutely no sense of humor.

The two women look at her in surprise.

This surprise gradually changes to puzzlement, because, although fully clothed, there is something slightly "off" about
Kate's appearance. We and they will realize that she is wearing her dress inside out. Kate never becomes aware of this)

Uh—Kate and I decided that our differences were undermining the
—uh, creative process, so I invited her over so we could discuss our
problems frankly and arrive at a reasonable solution.

KATE

And, of course—as always happens when two human beings reach
out to one another—it worked.

JASON

The point is, we discovered that we're both after the same thing—
the best possible production. We've just been coming at it from two
different places.

(Kate notices Phoebe peering at her in a dazed manner)

KATE

Is there something the matter?

PHOEBE

What? Uh, no.

KATE

I sense some bad vibes in the room.

BLANCHE

It's probably the radiator.

JASON

Would you care for a drink?

KATE

No, thanks. I stopped four years ago when I woke up in a motel room with those four jockeys and the Vice President.

(There is a pause)

BLANCHE

(Finally)
Who were the jockeys?

(The other three turn to look at her. She shrugs)

I'm not political.
(Kate moves downstage for her coat, revealing a fairly large label on the back of her dress. Now even Jason is aware of the way she is dressed)

KATE

I can't seem to find my coat.
(She turns, notices the other three staring at her)
Why is everyone staring at me?

BLANCHE

(Finally)
Star quality?

(Jason picks up her coat, quickly moves to her, holds it up for her to put on)

JASON

Here's your coat.

KATE

I'll carry it, thanks. Should I call a cab or can someone give me a lift?

BLANCHE

My car's outside. Where can I drop you?

KATE

At the park. I'll walk the rest of the way.

(Blanche moves to get her coat)

BLANCHE

(Just making conversation)
Are you enjoying your stay?

KATE

(With a sweet smile)
Oh, I just love New York. Every time I come here, I feel like going down on the whole city.

(There is a moment's embarrassed pause)

BLANCHE

Well, you certainly have the weather for it.
(A beat)

KATE

I want you to know a beautiful thing happened this afternoon. Two human beings made contact. Now let's go to work!
(She exits. Blanche shoots an incredulous look at the still stunned Phoebe and exits. There is a small, tense pause)

JASON

Yes—well—
(Avoiding her eyes, he moves briskly to the desk and picks up some script pages)
We need to take ten minutes out of the play. Nothing in life should last longer than two hours.
(Phoebe, who hasn't moved, clears her throat)
We also need a new curtain line for scene four. You have any ideas?

(She doesn't answer, but clears her throat and stares straight ahead)

Phoebe, are you going to stand there making raspy, little noises or are we going to work?

PHOEBE
(Tightly—a touch of the schoolteacher)
It's no good you know.

JASON
What isn't?

PHOEBE
We all noticed, Jason. That woman had her dress inside out.

JASON
(Flustered)
So, she's sloppy. You should be able to identify with that.

PHOEBE
Her label was showing!

JASON
(Uncomfortably)
Phoebe, we have a lot of work to do here.

PHOEBE
(In a dry, strained voice)
You went to bed with her, didn't you?

JASON
You want me to stand up and share it with the rest of the class?

PHOEBE
Don't deny it.

JASON
Look, do you want to fix this play or not?

(She stares at him, absolutely stunned, her worst fears
confirmed)

PHOEBE
My God, how *could* you!!

JASON
Well—it wasn't easy.

(She is staring at him, her eyes welling up with tears)

Phoebe, I didn't commit an axe murder! Why are you staring at me like that?

PHOEBE

It's—it's so—unprofessional!

JASON

Actually, it was *very* professional.

PHOEBE

(Tightly—moving away)
Well, I'm glad she has some technique *somewhere.*

JASON

What I mean was it *started* out as a professional thing.
(A trifle desperately)
Look, I did it for you too.

PHOEBE

(Icily)
Did I enjoy it?

JASON

I was just trying to—improve my relationship with her.

PHOEBE

(Exploding)
Oh, don't try to romanticize it! You've been *cheating!!* You committed adultery!

(He stares at her)

JASON

You know, I don't believe this. You sound like a *wife.*

PHOEBE

(Still angry but flustered)
I happen to be a friend of your wife.

JASON

It's not the same thing.

PHOEBE

I'm your partner!

JASON

Exactly. You're not my priest, you're not even my mistress—and my private life is none of your business.

PHOEBE

I don't care what you do in your private life, but—but you did it right here—in our *office*—where we *work!*

JASON

Phoebe, it's not a cathedral. Now what the hell is the matter with you?

PHOEBE

I thought I was working with a man of honor.

JASON

Did I ever say or do one thing to make you believe that?

PHOEBE

You said you wanted to keep your teapot intact!!

JASON

Oh, for God's sake—you sound just like a woman.

PHOEBE

(Tightly)
It's one of my best impressions.

JASON

Yes, that's always been the problem.

(She looks at him)

Well, if you were a man you wouldn't be carrying on like this. We wouldn't even be *talking* about it. At least not in the same way.

(She doesn't say anything)

We'd have a couple of laughs and forget it. You'd cover for me. You'd be a pal—a buddy.

PHOEBE

(Finally)
I find that—revolting.

JASON

Look, what exactly would you like me to say?

PHOEBE

I'm trying—very hard—to understand your actions.
(A beat)
Do you love her?

JASON

(Incredulously)
Love her? I can't even hear her from the balcony!

PHOEBE

Then *why*?

JASON

Oh, for God's sake, don't you understand *anything* about sex?

PHOEBE

Evidently not.
(She is having trouble controlling her tears and moves to get her coat)

JASON

What are you doing?

PHOEBE

Leaving.

JASON

All right, I know it's been a long day.
(He sits with pages of script)
I'll work on the cuts and tomorrow we can concentrate on the—

PHOEBE

I mean permanently.

(He looks at her as she stamps her feet into her boots)

JASON

Are you serious?

(She doesn't answer)

You'd actually walk out on a ten-year partnership over something so stupid and trivial as this?

PHOEBE
(In a strange voice)
Goodbye, Jason.
(She moves toward the door and opens it. Just as she is about to exit, Jason, not looking at her, speaks quietly)

JASON
Did you know I had my nose fixed?

(She stops. Finally, her curiosity gets the better of her. She turns)

PHOEBE
What?

JASON
My nose. It's fixed. I had it done years ago.

PHOEBE
(Bewildered)
What has that to do with—

JASON
I'm trying to explain why this afternoon happened.

PHOEBE
(Baffled)
She found out and blackmailed you into going to bed with her?

JASON
My teeth are capped, too.

PHOEBE
I really don't understand why—*all* of them?

JASON
(Irritably)
No, not all of them! Look, will you stop interrupting? I'm trying to make a point. Please sit down, and hear me out. After ten years, you at least owe me that.

(After a moment, she closes door, sits and waits. Jason starts speaking, not looking at her)

My real name isn't Jason Carmichael. It's Joey Mahovalich. I didn't graduate from Yale—I never even finished high school. I grew up, a fat little kid with a bad nose and a worse accent on 12th Street in the South Side of Detroit. Did you ever notice I have no relatives? My father wasn't a lawyer—he worked for the Gas Company. I never knew him—he ran off with a woman who lived upstairs when I was four years old. My mother took a job in the cafeteria at the G.M. plant so I lived pretty much on the streets. She died when I was thirteen and I was put in a series of foster homes. I was arrested three times before I was fifteen for stealing—mostly food from vending machines.

(He looks at her)
Do you know who I really am?

PHOEBE

Oliver Twist?

(He doesn't smile. She makes a gesture of "forget that")

JASON

I'm a totally manufactured man. I didn't like my life, hated what I was—so I became someone else. You know why I married Allison? I couldn't get over the fact that a girl with her background would want someone like *me*. But she did. My God, now I had the "right" wife. So there I was—the successful, urbane playwright—the host of the most glittering dinner parties in town. Fooled a lot of people; but *I* never believed it. Inside the Saville Row suits there was always the ugly, fat little kid waiting to be found out. So much for the past. Lately, I've been feeling more—unattractive than usual. Things between Allison and me haven't been—Look, I'll be forty-six next month. Middle age. Pick your cliché.

(She remains silent, her face impassive. Finally)

And none of that is the real reason this happened. I was angry at you—because of Leo. I suppose—in some way—I wanted to lash back.

(She is too astounded to say anything. A pause)

All right. I was terrified of losing you. So you see before you an inse-
cure, middle-aged man who just this afternoon made a complete ass
of himself and couldn't regret it more.

PHOEBE
They did an incredible job on your nose.

JASON
Is that all you have to say?

PHOEBE
Look, you've given me some understanding of why you did what you
did. But, right now, I'm still not too fond of you.

JASON
Well, that makes two of us.

> (She takes her hat, gloves and scarf off and picks up the
> script he has been working on from the coffee table)

PHOEBE
I think you may have cut too deeply here. The last line contains the
right set up for the Act One curtain line.

JASON
Is class dismissed, Miss Craddock? I've been thinking about the end
of the play. I think I have the solution.

PHOEBE
Good. Now all we have to do is come up with the problem.

JASON
Phoebe, it's all too neat, too slick. You know what I mean?

PHOEBE
Yes. Professional.

JASON
Pat.

PHOEBE
(Warily)
What do you have in mind?

JASON

Well, it's not clearly formulated in my mind yet—I'm just thinking out loud—but supposing she doesn't stay with the lover *or* return to her husband?

PHOEBE

That only leaves the seventy-five-year-old gardener.

JASON

(Doing a very good acting job)

I don't know—I just have a gut feeling about it. Wait a minute— why does she have to end up with anyone? I mean this is 1975. It'll give it a more contemporary feeling.

PHOEBE

You mean "make her a Joan of Arc of the seventies."

JASON

What a good idea.

(Phoebe throws the script at Jason, exits briefly to the dressing room and returns with a battered suitcase. She throws it on the ground, opens it)

What are you doing?

PHOEBE

Packing!

JASON

Because you don't like my idea for a second act?

(Falsely jolly)

Really, a simple "no" would be sufficient.

(During the following scene Phoebe gets various articles from around the room and throws them into the case.

The articles include a portable typewriter, a number of books, scripts, assorted objects from the desk drawers, sneakers, etc. Her "packing" is noisy and punctuates some of her remarks)

PHOEBE

No, it wouldn't.

JASON

Oh, come on, Phoebe. You've lost all sense of proportion.

PHOEBE

(Exploding)

And you've lost your integrity!! You've sold out to that woman!!

JASON

One sell-out and I've lost my integrity? Look, do you know what you're doing?

PHOEBE

I'm getting married, going to Paris, and having three children.

JASON

But you can't leave right now! We have a play in rehearsal!

PHOEBE

Send me the reviews.

JASON

That's not good enough, damn it! You have responsibilities here.

PHOEBE

I'm sure you and Kate Mallory can take care of any rewrites.

JASON

I'm not talking about the play. What about the children?

PHOEBE

I'm not their mother.

JASON

You're more than their mother. You *like* them. You listen to them.

PHOEBE

Well, maybe if you'd been the father you should I wouldn't have had to spend so much time with them.

JASON

Wait a minute—there has to be more to this than an artistic difference of opinion. Just what is bothering you, Phoebe?

(She stops packing, looks at him)

PHOEBE

Bothering me? All right, I'll tell you what's "bothering" me. I don't like you anymore! You're a vain, arrogant, insensitive, selfish bully!

JASON

I am not vain!

(She stabs a finger in the direction of a chair)

PHOEBE

Then why do you always sit on that couch?

(Jason is nonplussed)

You know why? So you can look at yourself all day in—
(Pointing at mirror)
That mirror! I think you're about to get an idea but you're *admiring* yourself!

JASON

(Coldly)
Is that all?

PHOEBE

No, it's not all. Whenever we eat in a restaurant you always take the best seat with your back to the wall so everyone can see you!

JASON

And so they can't see you! You dress like a walking garage sale!

(She stops packing to look at him)

PHOEBE

My father has a word for people like you—"jerk"!

JASON

I see your gift for language runs in the family.

PHOEBE

You said you liked my father.

JASON

I lied. Your father is a boring, illiterate, old poop!
(Pointing at book she is holding)
Wait a minute—that was given to both of us!

PHOEBE

It was given to me!

JASON

Read the inscription!

PHOEBE

Oh, keep the damn book!
(She throws it at him and it hits him in the chest)

JASON

You could have broken a rib! I mean just who do you think you are?

PHOEBE

(Hysterically)
I'll tell you who I am! You're full of shit—that's who I am!

(He is too astounded to reply.

She goes back to packing)
God, I'll be so glad not to have to face you every day!

JASON

(Angered)
You think it's been easy living with your relentless perkiness all these years? Have you any idea how depressing it is to be around that much—niceness?

PHOEBE

(Thrown)
Niceness is depressing?

JASON

Mealy-mouthed niceness! Like that time when that actress propositioned you. She asked, "Are you gay?" and do you know what you said?

PHOEBE

(Puzzled)
I said, "No, I'm not."

JASON

No, you didn't. You said, "No, I'm not—*but thank you for asking!!*"

(At this point Allison enters but stops when she sees what is going on. Neither Jason nor Phoebe notices her)

You're afraid of offending anyone!

PHOEBE

Yes, well, maybe that's why I say "goodbye" when I leave a room and "hello" when I come in.

JASON

Very original.

PHOEBE

You *never* say "hello" or "goodbye." You just leave. It's the ultimate conceit!

JASON

Better than your stammering, blushing humble act. Let me tell you something—you're not talented enough to be that humble!
(At this point he notices Allison.

Phoebe also turns and looks at her.

They watch her as she tiptoes across the room, picks up some mending from Phoebe's corner downstage right. She tiptoes back to the door)

ALLISON

I'm sorry. I didn't realize you were working.
(Allison exits.

Phoebe picks up a staple gun, holds it up)

PHOEBE

This is mine.

(Jason moves to the desk)

JASON

Here, you want to take some paper? You want half the pencils?
(Throwing objects from the desk)
Paper clips? Used typewriter ribbons? Wait a minute—there's half a box of Kleenex in the dressing room!

PHOEBE

I'm walking out of here with exactly what I came in with!

JASON

Plus fifty per cent of my royalties!

PHOEBE

Which I more than earned!!

JASON

And from which you have the first nickel—plus towels and soap from every hotel we ever stayed in. You know what I really despise about you? I loathe your—

PHOEBE

Cheapness.

JASON

Your finishing my sentences for me!

PHOEBE

Someone has to do it!

JASON

(Infuriated)
You really want to know what I've always really hated about you?

PHOEBE

Why not? You've gone this far.

JASON

I've always hated your ass!

PHOEBE

Eloquent. Very eloquent.

JASON

I mean, I *literally hate your ass!!* You and your damned exercises! Every morning for ten years I turn around and find I'm addressing your rear end. Believe me, it's not a pretty sight.

PHOEBE

(Hurt—fighting back the tears)

Yes—well—I think I'll get a second opinion on that. Goodbye, Jason.

JASON

Phoebe, you can't leave.
>(A last desperate plea)
I named one of my children after you!

PHOEBE

>(Finally—quietly)
It's not enough, Jason.
>(She goes to close the suitcase but it is so loaded it won't close. In a mixture of frustration and rage, she kicks the case)
Oh, to hell with it!
>(Phoebe takes a small tank of goldfish under her arm and crosses to the door)

JASON

It won't last three months! Once he sees those substandard flannel nightgowns he'll run for the nearest fire escape!

>(This really stings her. She turns around)

PHOEBE

>(With dignity)
I only have one reply to that. Even an egg takes three minutes.

JASON

>(Baffled)
What?

PHOEBE

>(Tearfully yelling)
You were inadequate in Chicago!!
>(She slams the door, leaving an outraged Jason. He crosses to the overstuffed suitcase and kicks it violently. It flies open and the impact has jolted the tape recorder and the music of "But Not For Me" fills the room. The anger drains out of Jason as he lifts the recorder out of the debris. He puts the recorder down when he notices her red baseball cap on the top of all the junk. He picks it up, crosses slowly to the sofa, finally puts on the cap and sits dejectedly)

JASON

Oh, Phoebe—you always were such a sloppy sentimentalist.

(The *CURTAIN FALLS*)

END OF ACT TWO

ACT THREE

Scene 1

TIME: Two years later. A mid-September morning.

AT RISE: The stage is empty. The room looks as if it hasn't been cleaned in weeks and is littered with old newspapers, magazines, dirty shirts, some jackets and trousers thrown haphazardly over chairs, paper coffee cups. The desk and tables are piled with scripts and mail, mostly unopened. Blanche, dressed for fall and carrying some containers of send-out food, enters, surveys the room with distaste.

BLANCHE
(Calling)
Jason! Jason, it's Blanche! Jason, I brought you some hot food! Jason!

(Jason, unshaven, wearing some wrinkled trousers, shirt, and an old, woolen cardigan, and looking very much the worse for wear, enters from the dressing room)

JASON
(Quietly)
Blanche, you're not in the Follies anymore. You don't have to be heard at the back of the house.

(She looks at him)

BLANCHE

You know if you expect your social life to pick up, you've gotta keep the phone on the hook.

> (He moves to bar. She picks up the phone and puts it back on the desk)

God, you look awful. Have you seen a doctor lately? I mean, you really look unhealthy.

JASON

Look, will you stop reviewing me if I give you a drink?

BLANCHE

It's only eleven a.m.

JASON

I have a watch, Blanche.
> (He pours himself a drink as she clears a space for food cartons during following)

BLANCHE

I don't know how you can live in this mess. Don't you ever have a cleaning woman?

JASON

A cleaning woman? Listen, I can barely afford to keep the Bentley.

BLANCHE

I still don't understand why you don't sell this place or at least rent out the two top floors.

JASON

Blanche, I'm simply going through a dry spell—I'm not quite ready to open a boarding house yet.

BLANCHE

Two years isn't a dry spell—it's retirement.

JASON

I've had a few distractions.

BLANCHE

Okay, you were upset when Phoebe left—I can understand that. I could even understand when you were divorced and didn't draw a sober breath for a year. What I don't understand is why you and the typewriter have become natural enemies.

    (He looks at her, sighs)

JASON

I tried, my love. Believe me, I tried but—
    (He shakes head)
—it's just—too damned hard.

BLANCHE

You don't even read the scripts I send you. You know that last play was by a young writer who's had three Off-Broadway productions that got very good reviews.

JASON

    (Mildly)
Blanche, just because he's never had a commercial success doesn't necessarily mean he's talented.

    (She looks at him for a moment)

BLANCHE

Why did you tell that man from CBS you'd only write for TV if your children got rickets?

JASON

I was trying to let him down easily.

    (She hands him a carton of soup)

BLANCHE

Here, drink this soup.
    (She watches him as he gingerly tastes soup)

Have you read Phoebe's novel yet?

JASON

Novel?

BLANCHE

Oh, come on, Jason—it's been on the best seller list for weeks. Five major studios are falling over themselves trying to buy the movie rights.

JASON

Please, I'm trying to eat.
        (He puts down soup, gets up, moves away to find cigarette)
If you don't mind, I'd rather not listen to the dubious accomplishments of a woman who ruined my life.

BLANCHE

What did Phoebe ever do to you?

JASON

She's a literary opportunist. She drained me dry and then she left me.

BLANCHE

        (Incredulous)
She got married.

JASON

Exactly. You don't get married and then have a best seller suddenly pop out of your head. She must have been hoarding the idea all the time we were partners. That's like a wife secretly siphoning off your money into a Swiss bank account.

BLANCHE

You said she ruined your life.

JASON

She caused my divorce.

BLANCHE

        (Surprised)
How?

        (He looks at her)

JASON

For that you'll have to wait for my memoirs.

BLANCHE

She's back in town.

JASON

Who cares?

BLANCHE

They arrived three days ago. Leo managed to get himself assigned back here so Phoebe could publicize her book.

JASON

How is she?

BLANCHE

You can see for yourself. She's due here any moment.

JASON
(Alarmed)
I don't want to see her. I'm not ready for that yet.

BLANCHE

When will you be ready?

JASON

When I have three hits running on Broadway.
(He picks up phone, holds up receiver)
Here—you'd better stop her.

BLANCHE

Why?

JASON
(Impatiently)
Because I don't want her to see me like this with my hair in curlers wearing a cheap kimono!

(Blanche hasn't moved. He puts the receiver down on the desk and moves to get his raincoat)

Anyway, I have appointments all day.

BLANCHE

Will you take some advice from an old broad who loves you like a mother?

(He looks at her)

When you see her, don't put on airs. You're much more appealing when you're vulnerable.

(He grabs raincoat and starts for the door but stops as Phoebe enters. She is impeccably groomed and coiffured and looks absolutely stunning in a chic, designer suit. Her manner has also changed and she projects an image of confident sophistication. They look at one another for a long moment)

PHOEBE

(Finally)
Hello, Jason.

JASON

Hello.

(There is a pause. She looks around the room)

PHOEBE

I see you've redecorated.

JASON

I see you have, too.

PHOEBE

Oh, I took off my glasses and let down my hair. Works every time.

(She is looking at him, trying to hide her surprise at his appearance)

JASON

I know. I look awful.

PHOEBE

(Easily)
I wouldn't say that.

JASON

Neither would I, actually. Blanche said it.

BLANCHE

Well, look at him. His skin has an unhealthy pallor, his face is all rumpled and I'm sure his liver is the size of the Palladium.

JASON

Nothing left but to shoot me.

(As Blanche heads for door, panicky at being left alone with
    Phoebe)
Where are you going?

BLANCHE

To make some coffee.

JASON

Oh, sit down. You don't even know your way to the kitchen.

BLANCHE

It's easy. I just keep walking until the floor gets hard and cold and if
I look up and see a lot of white furniture, that's it.
    (She exits. There is an awkward pause)

JASON

How's Leo?

PHOEBE

Fine. He's out apartment hunting right now.

    (Jason nods)

Oh, Timmy and little Phoebe send their love.

JASON

You saw them?

PHOEBE

We drove up to Tarrytown for the weekend.

JASON

How's Allison?

PHOEBE

Very well. I suppose you know she's running for Congress.

    (He nods. A small pause)

You live alone?

JASON

All alone.

    (A small pause)

PHOEBE

I'm sorry I walked out on you, Jason. I mean at that time—in the middle of a production.

JASON

It wouldn't have made any difference if you'd stayed. Nothing could have helped that play.
(He frowns)
And, since we're on that subject, I said a lot of things in the heat of anger before you left that—

PHOEBE

You don't have to apologize for—

JASON

No, no—there's something I said that's really been bothering me and I'd like to retract it. It was stupid and childish and I should never have said it.

PHOEBE

What?

JASON

I never had my nose fixed.

PHOEBE

I know.

JASON

How?

PHOEBE

It was out of character.

JASON

For me to have it done?

PHOEBE

No, for you to admit it.
(He gives her a wintry smile)

JASON

I'd forgotten what an excellent judge of character you were.

PHOEBE

Why are you nursing such a grudge?

(He turns to face her)

JASON

You're asking that seriously?

PHOEBE

It's rather important we clear the air.

JASON

Why?

PHOEBE

You'll understand later. All right, I admit I left you at an inopportune time—but is that any reason to go into a childish sulk?

JASON

Childish? You turned my life upside down, you ruined my marriage!

PHOEBE

(Puzzled)
How did I ruin your marriage?

JASON

(Evasively)
Look, I really don't see any point in rehashing all this.

PHOEBE

In what way did I ruin your marriage?

JASON

All right! Do you know why Allison left me?

PHOEBE

She found out about you and Kate Mallory.

JASON

And how do you think she found out? Why do you think she kept her nose to the scent like a Tennessee bloodhound?

PHOEBE

I have no idea.

JASON

Allison kept asking me why you'd walked out and wouldn't accept any of the reasons I gave her. It was maddening. She said for you to leave me I must have done something absolutely horrendous.

PHOEBE

Why did she think that?

JASON

Look, she was quite demented at the time—totally irrational—it made no sense at all.

PHOEBE

What didn't?

JASON

She said that all the years you and I were together you'd been in love with me.

PHOEBE

I was in love with you.

JASON

Well—now you can see why I bear you a certain—animosity.

PHOEBE

No, I don't.

JASON

For God's sake, you might have had the decency to tell me!

PHOEBE

You were married. You know what a stickler for form you were.

JASON

(Uncomfortably)
Well, you certainly kept it hidden very well.

PHOEBE

(Calmly)
Allison knew.

JASON

Yes—well, I don't know how she sensed that.

PHOEBE

Maybe it was the way I hung on every word you said and started to
perspire when you came within two feet of me.

JASON

I have that effect on a lot of people.
        (He sits)
Anyway, I resent being the last to know.

PHOEBE

You were the first, Jason. You always knew and you enjoyed it. Oh,
I can't say I blame you. You had the best of everything. Two
women who adored you and had devoted their lives to satisfying
your every whim.
        (She turns to look at him)
And you revelled in it.

JASON

Did you come up with that idea all by yourself?

PHOEBE

No, I went into analysis.

JASON

Why?

PHOEBE

You're an arrogant, often unfeeling, difficult man and yet for some
ten years I was totally infatuated by you. I am now married to a
nice, sensitive man and if my marriage was going to work, I believed
it was important to come up with the reasons for my relationship
with you.

JASON

        (Quietly)
Why do you think I'm unfeeling?

PHOEBE

Jason, do you know that the only time I ever saw you cry was when
a pit orchestra struck up? Never in real life.

JASON

Tears are simply the appearance of emotion. Not emotion itself.

PHOEBE

You mean you could be feeling something but it's for you to know and everyone else to find out?

JASON

What other blinding revelations did you experience?

PHOEBE

That when I found out about you and Kate Mallory I was angry with you because I really wanted you to make love with me.

JASON

You know, I liked you better before you came out of your shell.

PHOEBE

It's not easy for me to stand here and say these things, Jason.

JASON

It's not a lot of fun where I'm standing either. Look, is this encounter part of your therapy?

PHOEBE

Partly. Naturally, I wanted to find out how I would feel when I saw you.

JASON

How's it going so far?

PHOEBE

Are you just being flip or do you really want an answer?

JASON

You used to be able to tell.

PHOEBE

I also wanted to see you for professional reasons. Have you read *Romantic Comedy*?

JASON

What's that?

PHOEBE

It's the title of my book.

JASON

I'm sorry, I've been rather pressed for time lately.

(She looks at him)

Well, don't look at me as if I haven't completed a homework assignment. I simply haven't got around to it yet.

PHOEBE

I thought you might be curious. No matter. I want to adapt it into a play and I want you to collaborate with me on it.

JASON

Why?

PHOEBE

There are two reasons. First, I'd like to tell you how I got the idea.

JASON

Is that absolutely necessary?

PHOEBE

It was a funny quote by Hemingway.

JASON

Yes, he's always cracked me up.

PHOEBE

He said that he and a woman had been in love for forty years but whenever she was single he was married and when he was single she was married. He said "we were the victims of unsynchronized passion." That started me thinking about us. I really started the book as therapy. Of course, in the writing I fantasized the relationship to make it interesting. I suppose what I'm saying is that you should write it with me because I stole your character.

JASON

Isn't this where you came in fourteen years ago?

PHOEBE

Well, that didn't turn out too badly, did it?

JASON

You said there were two reasons.

PHOEBE

The second one should be obvious. You're the best dramatist of this sort of material I know.

JASON

There's a third reason.

PHOEBE

Oh?

JASON

You think I need the money and my life is a shambles.

PHOEBE

Yes—well, I'd be less than honest if I said I wasn't aware of that. But that has nothing—well, very little—to do with my offer. It's not your lack of money that worries me, Jason. It's your lack of spirit. You need to work.

(Jason slowly rises)

JASON

(Icily angry)
I am not a charity case!!

PHOEBE

I never said you were.

JASON

(Tightly controlled)
No, you said a lot more. Well, now let *me* say a few things. You come waltzing in here, clutching your tawdry little best seller and expect me to kiss the hem of your Givenchy dress! Well, you've made a few assumptions that need correcting. First, I may have been going through a somewhat fallow period but my career did not freeze into a "still life" the moment you left. I was writing plays when you were a teenage ticket taker and I suspect I'll be writing them long after you're a plump matron making funny speeches about your septic tank to the P.T.A. Next, your infantile psychological insights about my character and your infatuation with an unfeeling, insensitive older man. Well, I'm exactly ten years older than

you, which doesn't exactly make me an aging Caesar to your pubescent Cleopatra!

(She moves to get her things)

Wait a minute, I'm not through!

PHOEBE

I know. You haven't come up with a good exit line yet.

JASON
(Growing ever more angry)

Next, your concern over my alleged lack of emotion. How the hell can you presume to know what I feel or don't feel? How do you know that when you left I wasn't quite—bruised.

(She doesn't say anything.

He picks up her baseball cap, waves it in front of her)

Well, I kept your damned hat, for God's sake!!
(He throws hat away)

Of course, I was remembering a warm, vulnerable, compassionate, unique girl who used to blush, not the woman you've become! You know what you've become? You've become—CRISP! One of those confident, crisp fashion-plate bitches who think they know the secret of the world and I wouldn't work with you if you were a combination of Molière and Mary Tyler Moore!!

(Stung, her tears are now partly from anger)

And, since this is obviously the last time we'll ever see each other, I was not inadequate in Chicago! I happened to be drunk and when a man is drunk, he—uh—he—

(He suddenly doubles over, his face contorted with pain, gasping for breath)

PHOEBE

What is it?

JASON

You'd better—stick around. I—think—I'm having—a heart attack.
(He collapses rather theatrically onto the floor)

PHOEBE

Oh, come on, Jason. We did that in *Innocent Deception* and it didn't work well there either.

JASON

(Groaning)
Stay with me, Phoebe.

PHOEBE

Jason?

(He doesn't answer.

Uncertainly)
Jason, don't play the fool. This is not funny.

(He turns his head towards her, breathing with difficulty. The realization hits her that he is not faking)

Oh, my God!!
(She rushes to his side; frantically tries to find his pulse, races for a bottle of brandy, uncorks it, rushes back, kneels beside him, raises his head)
Here—drink this brandy!

JASON

(Feebly)
What—what year—is it?
(Phoebe is giving Jason mouth-to-mouth resuscitation when Blanche comes in with the coffee tray)

BLANCHE

Well, I'm glad to see you two finally got together.

PHOEBE

Blanche, he's not breathing . . . call an ambulance.
(Phoebe goes back to the mouth-to-mouth, Blanche goes to the telephone as the *CURTAIN FALLS*)

END OF SCENE ONE

Scene 2

TIME: Late afternoon, three weeks later.

AT RISE: Jason is propped up on a pulled-out sofa bed which has
           replaced the sofa, with a tray across his lap, yelling
           for Phoebe. He is wearing a robe and pajamas and is
           sporting a sling that supports his right wrist. The room
           has also been restored to its usual elegant charm.

JASON
(Calling)
Phoebe! Phoebe, I need you! Phoebe!

(Phoebe, looking harassed and somewhat untidy, enters carrying a pile of mail)

PHOEBE
I heard you the first time.

JASON
I need you to cut up my food.

PHOEBE
Tapioca?
(She puts the pile of letters on the desk)

PHOEBE
Here's your mail.

JASON
You can read it to me later.

PHOEBE

Jason, I'm not Annie Sullivan. It's bad enough that I have to feed you.

> (She takes spoon, feeds him through following)

JASON

Serves you right for trying to kill me.

PHOEBE

I was trying to save you.

JASON

You almost suffocated me.

PHOEBE

You should have said something.

JASON

I tried. That's when you fractured my wrist with your bony knee.

PHOEBE

Could you chew a little faster? I have about a million things to do.

JASON

You shouldn't overdo it, Phoebe.

> (She looks at him)

You're looking—I don't know—wispy.

PHOEBE

Eat.

> (Leo enters carrying a pile of telephone messages. He moves to the two of them, peers at Jason)

LEO

So what do you think? Will he ever tap dance again?

JASON

I'll never eat tapioca again. What are those?

LEO

Telephone messages. I feel like a bookie.

JASON

Why has the phone stopped ringing?

LEO

I left a message on your answering service that you'd died. Thought
it might slow 'em down.
>   (He stands, waiting. Phoebe looks at him)

PHOEBE

Something on your mind?

LEO

Sure. Dinner.

PHOEBE

>   (Annoyed)

You're waiting for me to make it?

LEO

>   (Evenly)

No, I'll make it. I just thought it might be nice to eat together for a
change.

>   (Phoebe is immediately contrite)

PHOEBE

Honey, I'm sorry. Give me about fifteen minutes.

JASON

Better make it thirty.

>   (They look at him)

Phoebe has to give me my massage first.

>   (Leo moves towards the door)

Oh, Leo, would you mind drawing my bath for me?

>   (Leo turns and looks at him. We hear front doorbell)

LEO

I have to answer the door and do the silver first.
>   (He exits. Phoebe starts to dressing room with two bed pil-
>   lows)

JASON

He seems a bit ticked off. Is he?

PHOEBE

Can't you tell?

JASON

Hard with Leo. He has a face like a totem pole. Probably his journalistic training.

(She looks at him but doesn't have a chance to answer as Blanche enters)

BLANCHE

How's "Camille" today?

PHOEBE

(Exiting to dressing room)
Oh, I think we can take him off the critical list.

BLANCHE

Jason, I brought the contract for you to sign. Have you read Phoebe's novel yet?

JASON

I'll try and get to it today.

(She looks at him)

Blanche, I'm recovering from a heart attack.

BLANCHE

A *mild* heart attack.

JASON

I know. But when your heart stops beating, it's inclined to bring you up short.

(Surprised at his seriousness, she regards him for a moment)

BLANCHE

You okay?

JASON

(Shrugs)

Something like this tends to make you reexamine your life. Decide what's really important.

BLANCHE

What is important to you, Jason?

JASON

Phoebe. She always has been—I've just never admitted it to myself before.

(Phoebe enters from dressing room carrying a portable massage table)

BLANCHE

You're giving him a massage?

JASON

There's a danger of my developing bed sores.

BLANCHE

You've been out of bed for days.

JASON

Well, we thought it would give me a psychological lift.

BLANCHE

Oh, we did, did we?
(To Phoebe)
You know what I think? I think your nurturing instinct has run amok.

JASON

Blanche, I'd appreciate it if you didn't come charging in here telling Phoebe how to run her ward.
(He exits to dressing room. Phoebe closes the sofa bed through following)

BLANCHE

Phoebe, I hope somebody is striking a medal for you somewhere. Beyond the call and all that.

PHOEBE

There was nobody else. Besides, I felt I owed it to him.

BLANCHE
How does Leo feel about it?

PHOEBE
It was his suggestion.
(Noticing Blanche's surprise)
Well, we needed an apartment and Leo's a practical man. Of course I don't think he realized just how demanding a patient Jason would be. He makes Sheridan Whiteside seem like a saint. That's the character in *The Man Who Came To Dinner* who—

BLANCHE
Honey, I know who Sheridan Whiteside is. I saw the original production.
(As Phoebe looks at her)
My mother took me.

PHOEBE
I'm sorry. When I talk to Leo I have to explain any theatrical references.

BLANCHE
What do you two talk about?
(Phoebe looks at her)
Well, you don't seem to have a lot in common.

PHOEBE
That's my fault, not his. I've led such a narrow life, really. It wasn't until I got to Paris that I realized just how frivolous, vain and self-absorbed people in the theatre are.

BLANCHE
Missed us that much, huh?
(Phoebe sets up the massage table)
Listen, don't you think all this is a bit dangerous? Rekindled passion, secret yearnings—all that good stuff?

PHOEBE
Blanche, you don't really believe you only meet one person who's right just once in a lifetime?

BLANCHE

In my case—even less. Listen, honey, I married three times. Once for sex, once for money and once for good conversation. None of them are what they're cracked up to be.

PHOEBE

What else is left?

BLANCHE

Beats the hell out of me.

> (Jason enters from the dressing room with Phoebe's book in his hand. He crosses directly to Blanche)

JASON

This book of Phoebe's is filthy!

BLANCHE

Are you trying to tell us you've never heard those words before?

JASON

It's not just the words. It's the sex passages. My God, they're positively pornographic!

PHOEBE

Jason, I was dealing with a young girl's fantasies about—

JASON

You really thought all those—things—about me?

PHOEBE

> (Embarrassed)

I really would prefer we keep this discussion on a professional basis. The girl—

JASON

The girl is *you*, Phoebe!

PHOEBE

The girl is *based* upon me. The *essence* may be me—all right, it is me—but naturally I embellished—

JASON

Why are you stammering?

PHOEBE

Because I'm extremely shy. Now will you take off your clothes and lie down so I can rub you?

(Jason takes off robe and pajama top and reading the open book, lies stomach down on the massage table)

JASON

Listen to this: "He had the lean hard body and supple legs of a tennis professional."

BLANCHE

So?

JASON

So that's *my* body she's describing.

PHOEBE

Don't be ridiculous, Jason. I didn't use your body.

JASON

(Coldly)
Oh? Why not?

PHOEBE

I wanted those passages to be erotic.

JASON

Well, it certainly *sounds* like my body—

(She is rubbing alcohol on his back)

—a few years ago. That feels good.

BLANCHE

(Picking up her coat, purse and briefcase)
Well, I'll leave you two alone to iron out your "creative differences." Oh, and Jason, try and be a better person.

(She exits. Phoebe starts to massage Jason's back as he reads)

JASON

(Reading)
"He was gracious, witty and elegant and wore the mantle of success as if it had been custom made." Well, you've certainly captured me there.

PHOEBE

I really wish you wouldn't read that out loud.

JASON

(Reading)

"But since he was stark naked I didn't become aware of these qualities until later. My immediate attention was caught by his—"

(She quickly pounds into his back)

Ooof!

(She continues massaging him and Jason succumbs)

Oh, that's better—oh, that feels good—yes, right there—Oh, yes.

(The door bursts open, Leo jumps into the room, and stands staring at them)

LEO

Ha-ha!!

PHOEBE

Ha-ha what?

LEO

(Deadpan)

I was outside the door and I heard these guttural groaning sounds and cries of pleasure. Naturally, I jumped to the conclusion that you were giving him a massage. So I burst in here—and sure enough you are.

(A beat)

So—ha, ha!

JASON

What do you want, Leo?

LEO

I have some things to do at the desk.

JASON

Well, we're trying to work. I mean you're not going to bang a typewriter, are you?

LEO

I'll use a soft lead pencil.

> (He moves to the desk, sits, takes some papers out and starts to work. Jason and Phoebe quickly forget he is in the room. However, Leo is very aware of the conversation and from time to time his head comes up from his work as he listens to them)

JASON

The ending bothers me.

PHOEBE

What?

JASON

The ending. It's too bittersweet.

PHOEBE

How would you know? You haven't read the book.

JASON

Oh, come on, Phoebe—I read the book when it was still in manuscript form.

PHOEBE

I thought so.

JASON

There are other problems.

PHOEBE

I know. Why does the girl stay in love with him all those years?

JASON

> (Sitting up)

Well, I could give you a few pointers on that. He's successful, witty, charming and never boring—at least not to her.

PHOEBE

But what about the audience? He may come off as arrogant, cold and heartless.

> (There is a slight pause. Jason looks at Phoebe)

I mean, for him to be sympathetic they have to know how he *feels* about the girl. After all, he never seems to return her feelings.

JASON

It wasn't that simple.
(A beat)
How about this? Supposing he's a man who believes in tradition—including the tradition of marriage. As soon as he marries he realizes he's made a mistake—but he's a honorable man so he lives with his mistake—the victim of bad timing. He makes the best of the situation.

PHOEBE

You mean he wants it both ways?

JASON

Look, it wasn't easy for me—him. Selfish, yes—but isn't that human?

PHOEBE

Not enough. I mean if he really loves her, why doesn't he tell her?

JASON

All right, maybe he's a man who has trouble showing his emotions, who likes his life—especially his emotional life—as tidy as possible. Not an admirable quality—not one he admires in himself, but ingrained in his character.

PHOEBE

Then why did he—

JASON

I can answer that.
(He sits, still not looking at her)
He had the affair with the actress rather than the girl—*because* she meant nothing to him. I—he thought it would keep the situation—emotionally tidy. If it happened with the girl he knew he couldn't control it—it would have blown the roof off.
(He turns and looks at her)
Do you believe that, Phoebe?

(There is a pause—finally Leo pounds the stapler, startling Jason and Phoebe)

What are you doing skulking back there?

LEO

I'm sorry to have interrupted you.

PHOEBE

Oh, you haven't.
(To Jason)
You don't want to work any more today do you?

JASON

No, I think we should call it a day.
(He moves to dressing room door, turns)
I feel we accomplished a great deal, don't you?
(He exits. Phoebe starts to fold up the massage table)

LEO

You need a hand with that?

PHOEBE

No, I can do it.

LEO

I'll do it . . . I'll do it.
(Leo takes table, looks at her)

PHOEBE

What's the matter?

LEO

It's amazing. Within three weeks he's got you back to looking like Cinderella before she went to the ball.

PHOEBE

I'm sorry, Leo. I know these last few weeks must have been very hard for you.

LEO

Just as hard for you.

PHOEBE

Well, I have been a bit distracted.

LEO

Distracted? I feel as if I've been living with a bad waitress.

PHOEBE

What do you mean?

LEO

I've been trying to catch your eye for days.

(She looks at him)

PHOEBE

You've caught it, honey. What's your pleasure?

LEO

When are we going to make love?

PHOEBE

(Flustered)
And I thought you just wanted to pay the check.

LEO

I'm thinking about that, too.

PHOEBE

(Finally)
Leo, I'm sorry, I—I just feel funny being in Jason and Allison's bed.

LEO

(Evenly)
I'm relieved to hear there's a good reason.

PHOEBE

I know it's silly but—there are a lot of memories in this house for me. Look, I've been exhausted lately.

(He doesn't say anything)

Leo, it was your suggestion that we move in here. You had to know I'd be run ragged for a few days.

LEO

Yes, I expected all that.

PHOEBE

Then why are you so upset?

LEO

You never have to ask each other questions.

PHOEBE

(Thrown)
What?

LEO

You read each other's minds. It's incredible. You finish each other's sentences like—like an old married couple.

PHOEBE

It's just an old habit, Leo. We've worked together so long that we're tuned into the same wave length.

LEO

It bothers me.

PHOEBE

Why?

LEO

Because you have to ask me why! For the past fifteen minutes I've been watching my wife and a man mentally copulate. I feel like a voyeur!

PHOEBE

Leo, you're exaggerating!

(Jason, now fully dressed, enters)

JASON

Listen, I've been thinking—
(He stops as he sees Leo and Phoebe staring at one another. There is a tense pause)
I have the feeling I've walked into the middle of a family squabble.

PHOEBE

Not at all. We—

LEO

As a matter of fact, you have.

(Jason makes no effort to move)

JASON

Well, don't let me interrupt you.
(Moving upstage)
I'll just sit quietly over here and read Phoebe's filthy book.

PHOEBE

We can talk about this later, Leo.

LEO

No, I think we're finished. I've decided to fly up to Rochester to see my kids.

PHOEBE

How long will you be gone?

LEO

I'll be in Rochester a few days—but I don't know how long I'll be gone.

JASON

Time for me to make a graceful exit.
(He starts for the door)

LEO

No, Jason. It's mine. I think you both should hear why I'm leaving. When I was about eight—don't panic, Jason, I'll cut it down to the highlights—I was a pretty fair stickball player. When the kids on my block chose up sides, I was always the second guy chosen. In high school I got straight A's. A girl named Stephanie Novak edged me out as Valedictorian. In college I was the second best distance runner in the state. The second. Are you following me?

JASON

(Quietly)
A pattern *is* starting to emerge.

LEO

Well, I've decided that this time I'm not going to settle for second. The others I could live with but this time I'd hate myself. And that wouldn't be fair. I'm a pretty nice guy and I don't deserve it.

PHOEBE

Leo—

LEO

(Quietly)

I'm almost finished. You see, it's not too bad getting the consolation prize but *being* the consolation prize really gets to me. I love you, Phoebe. I probably always will. But—I want my marriage to be a blue ribbon affair. Now I'm not exactly sure what is going on with you two—I'm not even sure you know either—but whatever it is, I think you should have a chance to find out and get it settled once and for all. To do that, you both need some time—and freedom.

(A beat)

That's about it.

(He looks at them for a moment and then moves to door and picks up his suitcase)

I wish you happiness—one way or the other. I'd like to say you deserve each other—but I'm not sure you do.

(He exits. There is a long, tense pause)

JASON

Well, he's right about one thing. He is a pretty nice guy.

PHOEBE

The hell he is.

(Jason looks at her in great surprise)

JASON

What?

PHOEBE

Who does he think he is handing me around from man to man like I'm an old football. Don't I have any say in my future?

JASON

Is that why you're angry?

PHOEBE

I'm angry because I can feel a tingling in my nose! Does that answer your question?

(Jason is too bewildered to answer)

This means I'm either going to sneeze or cry and I have the feeling it's going to be the latter. I don't want to cry, Jason. It's embarrassing to stand here and dissolve in a flood of tears in front of you. Because I'll be honest with you, Jason. I don't like you much either. I should be expressing pure anger but my ducts are filling up—and my vision is blurring and—

JASON

Phoebe, you're not a doctor experimenting with a new drug. You don't have to keep notes.

PHOEBE

Just leave me alone.

(He hands her his silk handkerchief)

JASON

(Awkwardly)
Here. If you must cry, at least do it in style.

(She takes handkerchief)

PHOEBE

I'll—I'll be all right in a few minutes. My marriage has just gone down the drain and I need a few seconds to compose myself before I start a new life. I know how you hate scenes but this won't take long. You'd better avert your eyes. I'm going to give in now and cry.

JASON

(Nervously)
Yes—I'll—I'll clear out of your way and wait over here.
(He moves upstage and sits at desk as Phoebe sits and cries.
Finally)
Feel better?

PHOEBE

Drier.

JASON

It's a start. Phoebe.

(She stops. He looks at her for a moment)

I missed the moment again, didn't I?
    (He stands)
You were right about my lacking spontaneity—one part of me standing back—always thinking of the effective gesture. And I did it
again.

PHOEBE

Oh?

JASON

When you were crying I should have taken you in my arms and
comforted you. I wanted to—but I was too busy considering
whether the staging was right—and the moment passed.
    (Incredulously)
Do you know what I said? "I'll clear out of your way and wait over
here." I actually said that. Do you know that I almost didn't give
you my handkerchief because it seemed cliché? What sort of man
would do that?

(She doesn't answer. He comes out from behind the desk)

Well, I don't know if the moment is right or not but—
    (He marches over to her, takes her in his arms and kisses her.
    They break, embarrassed)

PHOEBE

Well, I suppose some decisions have to be reached.

JASON

I suppose they do.

PHOEBE

What would you like for dinner?

JASON

Could we begin with something easier?

PHOEBE

I'll get it started.
    (She moves towards the door)
—I just think you should know—I don't have the faintest idea of how to go about this thing.

    (They are gazing at one another as the *CURTAIN FALLS*)

END OF SCENE 2

Scene 3

TIME: The next morning.

AT RISE: Jason and Phoebe are sharing the sofa bed. Jason is
                asleep, Phoebe, in his robe, is looking lovingly at him.
                Jason wakes and turns to her.

PHOEBE
(Finally)
So—how do you like your eggs?

(He turns to look at her)

JASON
You *know* how I like them.

PHOEBE
Scrambled?

(He nods. A small pause)

How did you sleep?

JASON
Fine.
(A beat)
How about you?

PHOEBE
Very well, thank you.

JASON

Good.

PHOEBE

Well—I'll get breakfast started.
>(She kisses him lightly, gets out of bed, picks up her clothes and moves to door)

JASON

You need any help?

PHOEBE

No, I can manage, thanks.

JASON

I'll tidy up the room.

PHOEBE

Good.
>(She smiles a trifle too brightly)

Well—
>(She rather awkwardly blows him a kiss and exits. Jason gets out of bed, calmly puts on his trousers and shirt. He is in the middle of buttoning up his shirt when he lets out a low, anguished moan)

JASON

That—was—the—most—*embarrassing experience of my life!!!*
>(He goes into the same maniacal dance we saw him execute in the first scene, jerkily moving around the room suffused with a combination of frustration and embarrassment)

God, that was—awful! Absolutely, utterly—horrendous! Humiliating! *The* most humil—
>(He stops as he sees Phoebe who has reentered and is staring at him. There is a pause)

I really wish you wouldn't keep doing that.

PHOEBE

>(Finally)

There's a hippopotamus in the room, isn't there?

JASON

(Uncomfortably)

Maybe if we ignore it, it'll go away.

PHOEBE

I don't think so.

(He looks at her)

Jason, I think we should discuss it openly and frankly.

JASON

What?

PHOEBE

Our—"you know" life.

JASON

Well, that's certainly being frank.

(She clears her throat)

PHOEBE

(Firmly)

All right. Jason, I don't want you to feel bad because I didn't have an orgasm.

(He looks at her for a moment)

JASON

Well, I don't want you to feel bad because I didn't have one either.

(She doesn't smile)

And as your cousin would say—ha-ha.

PHOEBE

Was it because of something I did—or didn't do?

JASON

(Uncomfortably)

Of course not. Why would you think that?

PHOEBE

Sometimes I get—overexcited.

(Somewhat baffled, he looks at her. She nervously clears her throat)

I mean I tend to have trouble accepting—the gift of sensuality and I get so anxious to please I come off as—an overeager puppy dog. You know, all wet tongue and wagging tail.

JASON

Sounds pretty good to me. Oh, Phoebe, it's not you—
    (Awkwardly)
Look, I think we're overreacting to the whole—situation.
    (He moves away to resume dressing)
It—it was fine.

PHOEBE

Fine?

JASON

Fine.

PHOEBE

    (Quietly)
Jason, after fourteen years and two wrecked marriages, "fine" doesn't quite make it.

JASON

    (Awkwardly—gently)
There was a lot of pressure on us to—succeed.
    (She looks at him for a moment)

PHOEBE

    (Briskly)
All right, let's try and put that in perspective first.
    (She pushes sofa bed in during following)
On a scale of ten would you say we're a five?

JASON

I can see why you were so popular as a teacher. You're an easy grader.

PHOEBE

Oh, my God.

JASON

What?

PHOEBE

I thought it was just me. I expected you to reassure me, tell me that it wasn't important.

JASON

I did.

PHOEBE

I didn't believe you.

JASON

I'm sorry, kid.

PHOEBE

(Finally)
It's funny, isn't it?

JASON

What?

PHOEBE

Us. Twelve years of pent-up passion and it didn't end with a bang—but with a whimper.

JASON

And very few of them.
(Gently)
We're about fourteen years out of sync, kid.

PHOEBE

Our timing's *that* bad?

JASON

We should have become lovers when we met—but that wasn't possible. So, over the years, I lived through your cold sores and you suffered through my post nasal drip. I held your head when you threw up on opening nights and you gave me sponge baths when I was sick. In short, my friend—we became friends.

PHOEBE

You don't think it's possible to have a good sex life with a friend?

JASON

I don't know. You're the first friend I've been to bed with.

PHOEBE
(Finally)
You know, after everything that's happened, after everything we've been through—people expect us to get married.

JASON

To hell with them. Let 'em find their own happy ending. That's the first time I've seen you actually *cry* at one of my jokes.

PHOEBE
(Tearfully)
It's just that we seem to have made such a mess of everything.

(We hear the front doorbell ring)

JASON

We're not the only people in the world with bad timing.
(He gets up, Phoebe moves to the door, turns)

PHOEBE

What are we going to do, Jason?

(They are looking at one another uncertainly as the doorbell rings again. She exits. Jason folds the sofa bed. After a moment Leo enters. The two men look at one another)

LEO
(Finally)
So how's it going?

JASON

Fine.

LEO

Phoebe's getting the rest of my stuff.

JASON

Where are you off to this time?

LEO

Spain. I thought I'd take some time off to write a book.

JASON

Why not? Everyone else is. Inside story stuff?

LEO

Fiction. Phoebe taught me a lot.

JASON

Do you regret having married her, Leo?

LEO

Of course not.

JASON

Do you mind if I ask you a personal question?

LEO

(Dryly)

I look on you as practically a member of the family.

JASON

How was your sex life?

LEO

(Finally)

You mean did the earth move?

JASON

Actually, I'd like you to be more specific than that.

LEO

Shouldn't we go into the locker room for this discussion?

JASON

Look, I'm not enjoying the tenor of this conversation, either. I wouldn't ask if it weren't important.

(Leo takes out his notebook and starts to write)

What are you writing?

LEO

Specifics. I thought if I put it in a questionnaire form it would be easier for you to refer to.

JASON

Sometimes I find your dry humor irritating.

LEO

(Still writing)

Did it ever occur to you that I might be embarrassed, too? Don't let these clothes fool you. I'm not as sophisticated as I look.

(Leo tears the page out of the notebook and hands it to Jason)

JASON

You're sure you're not exaggerating?

LEO

(A beat)

I'm only working from memory, of course.

JASON

(Caustically)

It's obviously extremely vivid.

LEO

Yes.

(The two men are staring at one another as Phoebe, now dressed, enters. There is an awkward moment)

PHOEBE

(Awkwardly)

So—what have you two been talking about?

LEO

Phoebe, you want to come to Spain with me?

PHOEBE

(Finally—shakily)

You think I just bounce from bed to bed like Nell Gwyn?

LEO

I think it's about time you grew up.

PHOEBE

How do I do that?

LEO

Come with me. Nothing's been lost, Phoebe.

PHOEBE

Oh?

(He shrugs)

LEO

Everybody has someone in their past they wonder about. All very romantic. But the very notion of romantic love demands that it be unrequited. So requited isn't what it's supposed to be. Things didn't turn out the way you'd planned. It happens to all of us.

JASON

(Agitated)

Look, if you've finished playing "the old philosopher." Aren't you assuming a lot? How can you possibly know it didn't turn out as planned?

LEO

(Losing his temper)

Because there's no way it could! Nothing could have lived up to the sort of expectations you both had!

JASON

(Rising)

Did it ever occur to you that we might just be in love with each other?

LEO

Oh, come off it! You're not in love with each other! You're in love with the magic of make believe!

JASON

Then why the hell did you leave us alone together?

(There is a slight pause as Leo regains control)

LEO

There was a good reason for that. Stupidity. It wasn't until last night that I realized how *stupid* I'd been. You had me playing a role —the noble husband who steps aside so that his wife can find "true romantic fulfillment." I mean what a bullshit thing to do!

JASON

(Mildly)
I thought it was rather a nice touch myself.

LEO

Is that supposed to be funny?

JASON

Well, I'm sorry if I'm not up to my usual form. You see I have this feeling I'm about to see a fourteen year old dream of mine destroyed. I've had it a long time! I've grown attached to it!

LEO

Yes, well I'm a reporter. I deal in the here and now.
(To Phoebe)
I'm not in love with the way you were fourteen years ago—or five years ago. I love the woman you are now—today. I want you exactly as you are.
(A pause)
Is it so hard to choose between us, Phoebe?

PHOEBE

(Shakily)
You're looking at a girl who couldn't even get a date on Saturday night. A very conventional girl.

LEO

Forget about conventions. Look, both Jason and I want what is best for you, but we can't decide that *for* you. Whatever you decide— we'll accept. For once in your life be selfish.

(She looks over at Jason)

JASON

(Finally—somewhat harshly)
He's right.

PHOEBE

(Hurt)
Don't you love me?

(He looks at her for a moment)

JASON

(Gently)

Phoebe, do you remember *Innocent Deception?* On paper everything seemed perfect but for some reason it just didn't work. The
chemistry wasn't there. It *should* have worked, we *wanted* it to work
but—it just didn't.

PHOEBE

(Tightly)

So much for happy endings.

JASON

Welcome to real life, kid. Take care of her, Leo.

(He moves away)

LEO

I'll get your things and grab a cab.

(Leo exits)

PHOEBE

If I walk out of that door it won't solve all our problems, you know.
All our lives—somehow we'll always be—connected.

(He turns to look at her)

JASON

Phoebe, you have a nasty little romantic streak in you that pops out
at the slightest provocation.

PHOEBE

Look who's talking.

(A beat)

And there's not an orchestra pit within miles.

JASON

Before you go there is something that should be said.

(A beat)

I love you, Phoebe. I always have. And when you came back and it
seemed you didn't feel the same way about me—I still loved you. I
suppose that was the clincher. I'm a very selfish man and the fact
that I could love someone without getting anything in return—

(A slight shrug)

Then when I woke up this morning—after everything had not been what we'd both wanted—you were still my best friend. I find that— extraordinary.

PHOEBE

(Finally)

So do I.

(Phoebe exits. Jason stands for a moment regarding the room. He moves up to the desk and looks again around the room. In the distance we hear the front door slam. Jason slumps over his desk chair. There is a pause and then Phoebe reenters)

PHOEBE

You're miscast as Sydney Carton you know.

JASON

Oh, I don't know. You're back, aren't you?

PHOEBE

Aren't you going to ask what happened?

(He turns to face her)

JASON

I know what happened. Friendship 1, Lust 0. Right?

PHOEBE

Well, I wouldn't put it *quite* that way.

JASON

How would you put it?

PHOEBE

I never quite got the hang of real life.

JASON

That's why you came back?

PHOEBE

No. Where else would I find someone as hopelessly outdated as I am?

(They smile at one another for a moment)

You working on the last scene?

                    JASON
Just doodling.

        (She moves into the room)

                    PHOEBE
        (Briskly)
All right. This couple have gone through the equivalent of a marriage. They finally get together only to discover the only thing they
have left is—what?

                    JASON
A mutual lack of passion.

                    PHOEBE
        (Quickly)
I'm very passionate about you!

                    JASON
        (Gently)
And I about you.

        (They look at one another for a moment)

We seem to be off the subject. They're left with—what?

                    PHOEBE
A mutuality of interests. They go to movies, museums, ball games
together. They grow old together—good companions. It's sweet.

                    JASON
It's depressing.

                    PHOEBE
It could be romantic—in a funny way.

                    JASON
Funny is good.
        (Jason crosses and sits on the sofa)

I've been thinking. Given the basic talent—and I'm sure they both have that—sex can be learned. I mean you weren't a very good writer when you came to me but, with a little instruction, look how well you turned out.

PHOEBE

If I run I could still catch Leo.

JASON

It would give them a common interest. Like learning a common language.

PHOEBE

Are you through?

JASON

I think so.

(Phoebe sits on sofa, taking Jason's feet on her lap)

PHOEBE

None of that is important. The important thing is friendship. I mean anyone can find a good sex partner. You found it with Allison. I found it with Leo.

(She is now stroking his leg under his trouser cuffs, too absorbed with what she is saying to realize the effect it is having on Jason)

But a true, loving friendship between a man and a woman where you accept one another's faults and still like the other—that's rare and valuable. *That's* what's important.

JASON

I agree.

PHOEBE

(Thoughtfully)
Of course it would be nice to have sex too.

JASON

Come over here, Phoebe.

PHOEBE

Shouldn't we keep working?

JASON

We'll improvise.

(She moves to lie down beside him, her head on his chest)

PHOEBE

I thought you hated improvisation.

JASON

I'm willing to learn.

(She is now moving into his arms)

It's not going to work with your elbow in my rib cage.

PHOEBE

Well, if you'd hold your head—

JASON

No—see, if you do that I can't breathe.

PHOEBE

No wonder this sort of thing always happens offstage.

JASON

It doesn't have to be a *ballet*, Phoebe. Just . . .

PHOEBE

Wait a minute—I have a better idea.

(She moves on top of Jason)

JASON

You really want to do it that way?

PHOEBE

Well, I think we should at least try it.

JASON

Yes, but it cuts off all circulation to my—knees!

(The curtain starts to fall)

PHOEBE

Jason, stop talking and—collaborate.

(The *CURTAIN FALLS*)

THE END